CAN
STEPFAMILIES
BE DONE RIGHT?

JOANN C. WEBSTER

SETH M. WEBSTER

CAN STEPFAMILIES BE DONE RIGHT?
by Joann C. Webster and Seth M. Webster
Published by Creation House
A part of Strang Communications Company
600 Rinehart Road
Lake Mary, Florida 32746
www.creationhouse.com

Unless otherwise noted, all Scripture quotations are from
the New King James Version of the Bible. Copyright © 1979, 1980,
1982 by Thomas Nelson, Inc., publishers. Used by permission.

Scripture quotations marked KJV are from the
King James Version of the Bible.

Scripture quotations marked NIV are from the Holy Bible, New
International Version. Copyright © 1973, 1978, 1984,
International Bible Society. Used by permission.

Scripture quotations marked TLB are from The Living Bible,
Copyright © 1971. Used by permission of Tyndale House
Publishers, Inc., Wheaton, IL 60189. All rights reserved.

Library of Congress Card Number: 00-111896
International Standard Book Number: 0-88419-674-7

1 2 3 4 5 6 7 8 VERSA 8 7 6 5 4 3 2 1
Printed in the United States of America

In memory of
"The loveliest lady in the land"
Nancy Corbett Cole

CONTENTS

1

WHAT IS YOUR VISION?

JOANN— I will never forget the ambivalence I felt while pacing a courtroom hallway when Seth was eighteen years old. I toyed with my pearls as I struggled for the right words to pray. *Lord, does Seth deserve to be locked up for five years? Will serving time help straighten him out? Or would he come out more embittered? If he isn't sentenced, will he think he can always get away with horrid behavior through his charm and wit?* As the minutes ticked by, I remembered the many, many days of in-school suspension and after-school detention, and although those seemed deserved, jail seemed a little much, even for a rotten stepchild.

I remembered some marvelous times we'd had together and some magical minutes we'd spent when he first came to live with us at the tender age of twelve. Coming home one evening, I saw Seth's slender frame silhouetted against our front door in the halos of porch lights. He looked so little, and it seemed cute that he'd been so grown up that night, going out without the family to an orchestra practice with his friends, one of whose mother dropped him off.

"Seth," I said in a loud whisper, hoping not to awaken the residents of our darkened street.

He bounded down the lawn toward me.

"Where were you?" he asked, as if happy to see me.

"I was at the Charter Hospital down the street. How was orchestra practice?"

"Fun," he said as we walked into the house.

"*Shhhh,*" I cautioned him. "Dad and Josh are asleep already. Are you hungry?"

We stole into the kitchen and turned on the low counter lights, then opened the refrigerator to pull out bread and our favorite, blackberry jam. It seemed secret and special, sneaking about the kitchen with him, whispering and eating our favorite food. He sat on the counter next to the toaster and, when it popped up, handed the toast to me to spread thick with jam. We filled the air with scents of toasted bread and sweet berries.

I took a seat on the counter opposite him, and we talked between bites. Light enveloped just the area around us, as if we were in a tent with a flashlight. What every stepparent hopes—to be accepted by his or her spouse's child—I felt was coming true for me. Seth told me all about his rehearsal and a kid named Ryan who played saxophone next to him. Their antics seemed charming, and I felt a tremendous sense of pride in his learning a musical instrument as well as being enrolled in honors courses. That's my boy!

He asked about my evening, so I told him a shortened version of the panel discussions of psychologists who had hosted an evening for community parents, titled "What Is Normal?" I'd gone because Seth's older brother, Josh, seemed intent on breaking every house rule. To discover what "normal" behavior or discipline should be, I had sought expert help. But the evening offered little because the psychologists had no different solutions from what my husband and I were already trying. I was placed in a discussion group with parents of teens, and each parent shared his or her story. I was the only stepparent there, which was strange to me. If biological parents were having this much trouble trying to find "normal," then what were all the stepparents doing? The entire group seemed moved by my story of trying to "blend" with my stepsons, and as one participant later departed, she said, "I'm going to remember you because what you're doing is a wonderful thing."

That night with Seth felt wonderful. After I told him a little about my evening and asked him about his, I ventured to ask him what it was like to live with us now instead of with his biological mother.

"I didn't care who got me when we went to court. I just wanted it to be over," he said, referring to the custody battle that had strained his loyalties to both parents. His stepfather was the reason the courts had given us custody. He was an angry man who took out his emotions on my husband's children. What happened in that home was characterized in court as "physical abuse" and "emotional abuse." I was foolish to press Seth about living with us and being away from that situation. My question could have made him uncomfortable. Such comparisons often don't come out the way the parent or stepparent hopes. But even as a child, Seth was analytical.

"It's like being on a plane," he said. "The plane is going to crash, but you don't know it. When it lands at your stop, you just get off, and you don't think anything. Later, you find out it crashed after letting you out, and you think, *I was lucky I got off when I did.*"

I took a deep breath. I was proud of his answer, even though it was far from the strokes I had thought I wanted. Seth had not known that his relationship with his stepfather was unusual because his mother had married his stepfather when Seth was only a toddler. Before we turned out the lights to go upstairs, I remember hugging him and telling him I was glad he got off that plane and lived with us. In shared moments like that, this child delighted me.

Six years later as I walked the tiles of the courthouse floor recalling that evening, many similar instances rolled through my mind. Although they didn't stack up in number against the almost daily skirmishes we experienced, they were far more memorable, and I was filled with compassion for this young felon who was my son. But where I once had expected to witness, perhaps, his inauguration into the White House, I instead was witnessing his all-out fight to remain a private citizen.

A wave of guilt made my shoulders shiver, and I forced back the nagging question of what part I'd played in where Seth ended up. Should there even be stepparents and stepfamilies? Were we too far out of God's will for Him to intervene in our lives? I knew that could not possibly be true. In succeeding years I proved to myself that nothing ever happened in our home that surprised God. It only surprised us.

We Can't Surprise God

Jesus had a stepfather.

For all that is said in praise of the nuclear family, God's Word is full of stories about blended families, fractured families, stepfamilies and horribly dysfunctional families—far more, in fact, than happily adjusted, biologically correct nuclear families, which we call *normal*. God sent His own Son to be part of a blended family. It appears that Joseph, the stepfather chosen for Jesus, was equal to the task and raised fine children of tremendous character without favoritism, even though one of them was indisputably perfect. Tough act for the other kids to follow!

Joseph, and even his wife, Mary, came from a long line of less-than-ideal families. Extended lifetimes, premature deaths and ancient customs, including polygamy, all contributed to the blended families in the earthly genealogy of Christ—and in the genealogy of most of our heroes of faith. Think of Abraham, the patriarch of three religions. Abraham's father incorporated his grandson Lot into his family, and in the next generation, Abraham had a child with his wife Sarah's maid, keeping the blending going. Jacob, Moses, David and Hannah all faced the challenge of surviving in blended families—the one they were raised in, the one they helped to create or both.

These biblical accounts of blended families range from horrid to beautiful. The scene where Jacob blessed his sons, birthed by four different women, is gripping. That he had a blessing for each son no one disputed, regardless of the child's parentage. Naomi passed on her family's blessing to her daughter-in-law Ruth, whom she mentored and advised. Ruth accepted Naomi's parenting and landed in the genealogy of Christ. Eli became a surrogate father to young Samuel, whom he parented better than his own sons. He blessed Samuel, and Samuel led the entire nation of Israel until his death.

This is not to suggest that the Bible *recommends* blended families. God's clear intention in Moses' law, which the apostles expanded upon later, is for a nuclear family to grow together, for a set of two parents to nurture and teach their biological children. We cannot take this to mean that members of blended families have an impossible task that falls outside the realm of God's authority and power—or His experience. The Word states that God hates divorce and that Moses granted divorce only because of the hardness of people's hearts. But when a marriage occurs after divorce or death, or when a child is placed in a home with someone other than a biological parent, God doesn't fall to pieces wondering what to do.

God has a plan for your blended family. He loves you and cares for you, knows what you're up against and understands your frustrations. In every situation, He already knows the way through it—even if you're the one who created the mess. I know this.

My stepson Seth and I experienced what seemed like fatal disasters in our attempts to "blend." It all culminated one night when he adopted a new nickname for me—"It." Yet we overcame every obstacle and emerged with a healthy, dynamic relationship. The entire experience built a stronger spirit in me by far, and it has become a tremendous source of fulfillment and personal satisfaction. Without Seth and his brother, Josh, my life would be anemic compared with the richness gained by the experience of raising them, which included tons of temporary grief.

Seth and I want to share with you how we blended, why we made certain choices, what worked, what didn't and when things came together for us. I've read books and studies that I'll cite, and we'll share our personal experiences, bathed in the almost divine light provided by hindsight. Seth's sections might be something you can read with your own children, to see if they feel the way he did. We believe that even though our story was a pretty wild ride compared with most stepfamilies, if you adapt the principles we learned to your own situation, then you also can survive and thrive.

More than anything, we want to encourage you to press on no matter how difficult it sometimes seems. We are living proof that even if you make a few wrong turns, God will fulfill His promise to make beauty out of ashes. When the Israelites fled Egypt and came to the barrier of the Red Sea, the path they crossed on was there all along. It was just covered by a big sea that God had to move. Even if you get a little lost in your family, or face a big barrier, there is a way for you, a path to freedom. God is no "respecter of persons," so we are certain that what He did for us and for the Israelites, He is just as willing to do for you.

As a Man Thinketh . . .

In one sense, our stepfamily was like all stepfamilies. All stepfamilies are formed out of loss, either through death or divorce. Loss can either swallow all hope of restoration or can itself be swallowed by new life. *The direction our families take depends on what we believe.*

At the tender age of eleven, I attended my first wedding with my parents. My father was a minister, and although we didn't have much materially, Mom always found a way to make us kids look good. I was excited to dress up for this special day.

Good ole Jack Jones, whose first wife had deserted him and their daughter, married Dolly, a beautiful young bride with glowing cheeks. I remember their emerging from a stone chapel with sunshine splashing over a green arbor at the end of a walkway lined by rice-throwing guests. Through whispered conversations I overheard, I discovered that Jack was lucky to have found Dolly and that he knew it. He even cried during the ceremony. No one said Dolly was unfortunate, but to my child's mind, I learned that forming a blended family was a tragedy disguised in a love story.

Twenty years later, after the divorce rate spiked, my husband, Richard, and I married on a balcony overlooking the sparkling blue Pacific, surrounded by lush gardens that pierced the heavy salt air with floral aromas. The waves crashing on the beach below became background music for a stringed ensemble playing Antonio Vivaldi's *Four Seasons*. The annual "tall ships" regatta provided silent entertainment as the ships glided down the coast in the cool autumn sunlight. Yet surrounding our picture-perfect wedding was an ominous, palpable border of negative emotion, and right there and then, on the happiest of days, I felt that strange anxiety I'd sensed as a child at Jack and Dolly's wedding. Another stepfamily had been formed.

As my husband, Josh, Seth and I "blended" through the years, it was always against a backdrop in my mind that nuclear "normal" families were "right." Even though I'd married the man of my dreams and God had directed our steps, the fact that he came with two children attached somehow seemed "wrong."

Perceptions are not always reality. But our perceptions are our reality. We may believe that God considers those of us in blended families to be less than His best, and therefore doomed to a substandard or otherwise difficult existence. But that belief, or anything akin to it, diminishes our belief in the power of God to deliver us from all our troubles.

As humans we cannot be perfect, which is why we need God. If we ascribe every flaw of a blended family to "The Divorce," and every problem our child encounters to "What Happened to Him Because of the Divorce," we'll pretty much ensure our own unhappiness—if not drive ourselves crazy. Because we all carry imperfections into every relationship we form, no relationship, not even that of a "nuclear family," can be perfect.

"For as he thinks in his heart, so is he."[1] God's overall will for you is clear. "For I know the thoughts that I think toward you, says the Lord, thoughts of peace and not of evil, to give you a future and a hope."[2] God desires peace for you and has a plan to fulfill your hopes. You are accepted by God, loved by God and forgiven by God, and His blessings will overtake your family regardless of prior gains or losses. But do you *believe* that? Divorced and widowed people alike often have anxiety and guilt rooted in the former marriage. Long after that marriage is over legally through divorce, or physically through death, a sort of "ghost" relationship continues with fear, anger, shame, jealousy or grief.

What Is Your Vision?

I recently met a man who reiterated what I've heard dozens of times: "If I'd known what would happen to my children, I'd have never divorced." Another friend said, "After seeing the dregs of divorce in my kids, I wish I could get down on my knees and beg my ex-husband to stop running around and to stay with me. I'd have no pride at all." Grief and repentance are important, but God never intended any of us to get stuck in them. *Guiltiness* and *godliness* are not synonymous. *As parents, we cannot afford to suffer so much over what we did to our children that we become incapable of doing what we can.*

Whatever may have happened, we must come to grips with our own culpability, with the rejection, bitterness, shame or fear, to keep those emotions from poisoning our thoughts—thoughts that keep us from believing we can have God's full acceptance, love and blessing in our new families. We must accept that God has a plan for our lives and our children's lives that didn't come unglued just because a nuclear family did.

Our family life starts with what we believe and with a vision. I believed my family was "wrong," yet I had a vision we could become "right" and act like a nuclear family. This was not the reality.

THE VISION

Samuel Johnson penned, "Remarriage is the triumph of hope over experience." We don't marry with the belief our marriages will fail. Most of us believe when we marry that, hope against hope, our marriages will thrive, regardless of any opposition against them. We create an image in our minds of how the marriage will survive and how the family will function. To the degree our reality differs from our vision, we become disappointed, resentful and frustrated.

The average couple in a stepfamily starts off without much of a

9

"honeymoon effect," and often questioning what on earth caused them to decide to marry. My friend, who married a man whose children lived with him, was shocked at how often she and her new husband found themselves running for their bedroom to lock the door behind them as if to defend themselves from alien invaders bent on destroying their happiness. Their first two years were tumultuous, filled with anger, frustration and hurt feelings that swallowed any chance of basking in the wonder of "togetherness." This is typical of a starting stepfamily.

omg!

A nuclear family starts with that honeymoon halo intact and the couple feeling very smug and content that they married. But as the years progress, the traditional marriage often fades from the heightened honeymoon stage while the marriage in the stepfamily increases in harmony. My friend's marriage thrived. She and her husband have a very deep, close relationship—one of the best I've ever seen. In general, stepfamily marriages that work *at all* work *very, very well.*

That's our good news—yet it is also our bad news. We believe we will have a very, very good marriage—yet if we expect instant happiness, then our expectations will collide with reality and we are bound to be rocked and rolled like my friend until the world settles down around us.

Each member of a blended family has expectations that differ from those of the others. Children's expectations are often different from adults such as biological parents and grandparents. Some stepparents believe they should take a proactive role. Others believe they should stay one step away, assuming an almost observatory role. Reconciling everyone's expectations, and choosing what role stepmembers will play, is crucial to settling in as a family.

A child's expectations are often the hardest to discern. In the "Good Father" syndrome, a stepparent chooses to "step in." But if the child feels this new relationship threatens his loyalties toward the biological parent, he'll jerk himself away. Or, a child who did not choose to have another parent can shun a well-intentioned stepparent from the outset. Or the child may not know that he or she can love more than one set of parents at a time. The child who is elated when the stepparent teaches him to dribble or drive or dress may have never expected the stepparent to do it so *well.* The child can resent the stepparent outdoing the biological parent. The undeserved anger that comes from a child's expectations or confusion can hurt both parent and step-parent.

Many problems are rooted in expectations that are based on a vision. Everyone has a vision. The most boring stick-in-the-mud's vision is that everything will remain the same, which is less than creative, but is still a vision.

HAVE A Vision!

Each of our minds has a vision of our marriage or family, whether that vision is spoken or not. The process of changing our vision is painful but necessary, especially in a blended family. The typical blended family re-creates itself several times before the child or children reach adulthood.

Compounding this problem is the cultural bias against stepparents. "Mean and wicked second cousin" has no ring to it. We all know the phrase is reserved for the stepmother because stepparents have the worst reputation in family life. Our society doesn't believe that grandparents are inherently evil—or uncles or great-aunts. But dating at least from the fable about Cinderella's "mean and wicked stepmother" to the present, stepparents in general have taken a beating. We members of blended families may have one vision for our families, but the rest of society—and other family members—often have a different vision, one based on the perceived "wickedness" of stepparents.

What is our vision? From what assumptions do our expectations spring?

CAN STEPFAMILIES BE DONE RIGHT?

OUR STORY

On a glorious autumn afternoon that smelled of damp grass and rain, my husband and I gained custody of his two sons in a sudden move by the court. On that day outside the Fort Worth courthouse I was filled with visions of our future. Abraham Lincoln once said, "All that I am or hope to be I owe to my angel mother," referring to Sarah Bush Lincoln, who became his stepmother when he was ten years old. Taking a cue from stepparents like her who succeeded, I felt certain my stepsons would like me and would one day say something nice about me. Yet at times, even this simple goal seemed unattainable.

My vision was larger than this, however, and unrealistic to a great degree—perhaps because I had watched *The Sound of Music* at least twenty times as a teenager and even more times as an adult. In the well-known story, a Roman Catholic novice, Maria, becomes a stepmother to the stern Captain von Trapp's seven children. If the real-life Maria was in any way as successful as the fictional Maria, I doubt that it came only from sitting up on stormy nights singing "Whiskers on kittens and bright copper kettles" or dancing on museum steps singing "Doe, a deer."

The idealized image of a stepmother in my vision was impossible to attain. Believing I could make a difference was realistic, but believing we could become the von Trapp family was a vision that could have killed our blended family unless it changed.

Each of us has to recognize our own vision. What are we expecting? Toward what goal are we willing to work? Is it realistic? What is our part in achieving that goal? We do well if we know the answers in advance of an angry stepchild, parent, spouse or grandparent asking, "Who do you think you are?" or "What do you think you're doing?"

An idealized vision that has a train wreck with reality sets off

12

reactions that can devastate a family. I never expected to struggle as much as I did with my stepsons because, after all, I started off like the fictional Maria singing, "I have confidence in confidence alone."

The day before Seth's court appearance, six years after he came to our home, we'd had sunny but brisk November weather. I had forgotten about Seth's hearing for a felony arrest until Richard had called me at work. By this time, the crises of being a stepparent no longer impressed me and had long ceased to impress anyone around me. To my friends, coworkers and family, I had become like the dreaded Aunt Mary who, right during the Thanksgiving dinner, wants to regale the family with stories of her last mammogram or the colostomy she almost had. Even sympathetic family members avoid sitting near Aunt Mary so they can eat a pleasant meal in peace.

The family and friends surrounding me were polite, but I had become certain they didn't want to hear any more about my kids' latest outbursts. My own mother never gave up on anyone—ever—but even she didn't seem fond of my stepchildren as subjects of conversation. Unlike Aunt Mary, I had started keeping my concerns to myself, so no one remembered we were going to court, including me. I suppose I had been disgusted with Seth, tired of dealing with him, somewhat angry with him, and I just didn't believe he would be locked up. He and his older brother, Josh, had always seemed to get out of what they most deserved.

I would pay for private schools or throw a big birthday party for one of my stepsons, and friends would say, "Why are you going to so much trouble?" I would always answer, "I'd rather do this than end up getting calls from jail one day." When the calls from jail had come even after all my hard work, I was more than a little disappointed. Like most stepparents, I felt their bent toward irresponsibility or crime was somehow a failure on my part. First one son then the other was hauled in, always for something minor like not paying a traffic ticket, until Seth was picked up for felony drug possession.

During long tear-filled nights I wondered what had happened. In long sessions of prayer, I talked with God about my boys and asked Him, *"Why?"* Why were my boys so prone to destructive behavior? Why was my life intersected with theirs? Why, after all my prayers, was I not seeing answers? And in moments of self-pity I asked God why He was doing this *to me.*

WHAT TYPE OF FAMILY DO WE CREATE?

Waiting to go into the courtroom for Seth's felony hearing, I looked down the hallway at my husband, Richard, smoothed the skirt I'd chosen for court, then readjusted the strand of cool, smooth pearls. I'd chosen my outfit in hopes of resembling Donna Reed and her television husband or the Cosbys with their darling children. Richard's dimpled chin and chiseled jaw matched Josh's, who sat on the other side of him. They looked similar to The Defendant who was sitting next to them, leaning toward a lawyer who spoke with great animation. I knew we looked good on the outside, but considering where we were, we were nowhere near the Cosbys, the von Trapps or the Donna Reeds. I couldn't help but think how differently our family had turned out from what I'd expected.

In a landmark study, Dr. James H. Bray identified three types of stepfamilies. One of these, the "Neotraditional" family, is the most successful because it is closest to "normal," meaning "nuclear."[3] It is also the closest to the biblical model in which a husband and wife share responsibilities based on mutual values. As the parents in a nuclear family raise the child, the father's and mother's values meld, and the family is defined as a unit. None of this "normal" melding is automatic in blended families. We have to work at it. In fact, stepfamilies have to work twice as hard as a nuclear family to get a fraction of the result.

The values held by each member of my family were so different when we started that even the simplest communication became a project. I knew what I was saying, but what my stepsons heard, and often what my husband heard, was different, filtered through their own sets of values and perceptions. But we had just enough value-sharing to develop a strong sense of "us," which is also a mark of a Neotraditional family. "Us" is a good thing.

Josh and Seth were living with their biological father, which is not the usual case because most blended families have a biological mother rather than father. The three of them talked about being "Webster men." Richard often reinforced this image in their minds, and it gave the boys a strong sense of belonging. Even when Josh and Seth descended into the lowest abyss of rebellion, they still felt some sense of pride at being "Webster men." I'm sure this was a crucial factor as they began to crawl up from the abyss and again become a part of the family.

My husband, Richard, is a former druggie-hippie of the '70s who became, oddly enough, a bit of a military junky. He enlisted in the Air Force during Vietnam, but was sent instead to Spain. While there, he and his first wife had the two boys, Josh and Seth. The family came home when Richard left the military, and he enrolled in college. In five years he received two degrees, in psychology and English literature—and a divorce. His wife took the boys, and he reenlisted, this time in the Army. The United States had just been involved in Grenada, and he had the "bug" for combat. He went through basic training—again—then jump school and joined the 82nd Airborne as an engineering specialist who would be first in combat, parachuting in to blow up bridges and prepare the way for the other good guys. But when it looked like the United States wouldn't be involved in any wars soon, he again sought a discharge and married me. Months later we watched on CNN as his 82nd

Airborne division parachuted into Panama. So Richard took up triathlons, weightlifting and target shooting—and reading and watching war stories.

The custody battle that delivered Josh and Seth to our home came three years after we married. From the beginning, the boys looked up to Richard as the embodiment of Sylvester Stallone, Arnold Schwarzenegger, Jean-Claude Van Damme and every other adventure hero combined. At ages twelve and fourteen, they needed a role model for their emerging manhood. It might have been their admiration for Richard's manly looks and masculine hobbies, combined with Richard's grasp of psychology, that saved us many times from unraveling as a family. The only way we developed close to a "normal" family likely started with that one value: the value of the "Webster man."

Another value we shared only somewhat was that of our faith, which was good. As one researcher puts it, "Families tend to be stronger and to do better when they share faith in something greater than themselves."[4] Our faith was a tie that strenthened over time. It was not, however, a magic wand that erased every other problem from the outset.

Dr. Bray calls the second type of family "Matriarchal," in which the family pretty much revolves around the mother.[5] She's the leader. Everyone else follows. Such families are most often formed when the children live with the biological mother. The father in such a family is often removed from decision-making in the activities of daily living, and the mother is competent and ambitious. He opts to be "one step away" and assumes little responsibility for the child. Matriarchal families can be successful, but have definite pitfalls.

A study from Columbia University found that mothers can better keep a child away from drugs by parenting alone than in a family where the father is there but disinterested in the child's life.

What Is Your Vision?

In a successful Matriarchal family, the father has to develop at least a "buddy" relationship with the child. The father would be active enough to monitor homework completion or play sports or games, even if he isn't tucking in the children at night or kissing and hugging them. Children need two active parents, even more so if two parents are in the home.

Then there's the deadly "Romantic" stepfamily, which those of us who watch too many old movies or *Brady Bunch* reruns try to inflict on our families.[6] In this idealistic stepfamily, the husband and wife believe they can become like a "normal" nuclear family. They expect an instant transformation at the wedding or the courthouse or wherever the family becomes a legal entity. As Miss Manners points out, ceremonies express ideals. They don't predict success. I think one reason I subscribed to the Romantic notion is because I was a Christian. I knew how to pray and believed God would answer. He did answer, but His answers came about seven years later than I expected.

Often Romantic parents also believe they have the luxury of acting normally around the children. The stepparent perhaps thinks criticizing or arguing with the biological parent is acceptable. Big mistake. Disagreeing with the biological parent in front of the children alienates stepchildren. I built up my husband in front of my children, and I saw almost before my eyes how such words could bring peace to the home. My accepting their father seemed to settle my stepchildren and cement in their minds that they were OK because their dad was OK, and together they were all Webster men.

For everything I did right, I did a lot wrong. The ideal in my mind and the first methods I employed were dead wrong. Although in the course of completing a social sciences degree I had taken plenty of psychology courses in college, I still thought I would develop a bond with my stepsons and help them overcome the life bumps of early

17

adolescence. I thought some kind of fast-fixing Super glue would turn us into a "real" family. Without having children myself, I perhaps rushed the situation with my new children, hoping to become a "real" mother. This is one of the big errors of stepparenting—don't rush intimacy with the kids!

Our "boys" are now adults and have just moved out—again—a change to which we all are still adjusting. Richard and I persevere with the finicky family cat named Tiger, who is now the "problem child" of the family. To get close to Tiger, we have to put our hands out, and maybe, just maybe, he will come over to sniff our fingertips. If he does, then maybe, just maybe, he'll let us pet him. He might even jump in our laps or crawl under the covers with us. He always does the approaching though—not us. And he will never come if we call.

Perhaps we put up with Tiger because his odd behavior seems familiar to us. A stepchild first has to get used to the fact that the stepparent lives there—and intends to stay. Then he or she may come around to get a better look and sniff out what the stepparent is like. These are necessary steps before the child is ready to be approached, and even then, the approach has to be with the utmost respect for the child's self-imposed boundaries.

Even if I hadn't rushed the relationship, the ideal I held created other difficulties. It is hard to hang on to a standard of behavior and level of living without imposing unrealistic demands on stepchildren. I had to refine and redefine my expectations while maintaining the vision, albeit a simplified version, of what I believed was basic, decent living. The fact that we did learn to live together with a good deal of harmony illustrates that even in the worst of circumstances an idealized view can become at least in some way a reality. But it does take time, which requires patience and a whole lot more. As one friend in a blended family put it, the field in front of a stepfamily's miracle is full of landmines, and as we seek to reach our miracle, we'll likely get blown up a few times.

SETH'S DAY IN COURT

By the time Richard and I walked into that courthouse for Seth's felony hearing, we had just celebrated our ninth anniversary and our sixth anniversary of living with the boys. The whole family lingered in the wide corridor outside the courtroom while Seth and his lawyer huddled on chairs that lined the walls. Even sitting, the tall Webster men towered over Seth's lawyer. Sunlight streamed through a window at one end of the hallway, and as I paced back toward it I could smell the warm dust floating in the sunbeams.

The first thing I had to do that morning, as I'd done hundreds of mornings before, was forgive my stepson. Seth was living at home at the time of his arrest, but it was Josh who called to tell me that Seth was in jail. According to Josh, he and Seth had gone with a friend to the local Target store. In the parking lot, some children on bicycles had yelled at them. Both Josh and Seth had hair-trigger tempers, so they jumped in their friend's car and started chasing the kids, who were on bicycles—on *bikes!* They stopped them in a nearby neighborhood. Hearing the fracas, a resident called the police. When the officers arrived, they discovered a large quantity of LSD in Seth's possession.

Local newspapers at the time were carrying front-page articles about the epidemic of LSD overdoses in our otherwise quiet suburb. The shocking part was, the drugs were being sold to school-age children, and the community was up in arms about it. I read the reports and hoped my drug-doing stepsons were not involved. But when Josh called to tell me Seth was in jail, and that his offense involved younger boys on bikes, I had to prepare for the worst—the newspapers were talking about my kids. My kids were the scourge of the community. My kids were corrupting everyone else's perfect, law-abiding, innocent children. The stepparent cannot escape the horrid feelings of responsibility no matter what the circumstances or how much our friends try to tell us otherwise.

Years earlier our friend Bruce, in casual conversation about his jailed brother-in-law, had said, "If his mother had never bailed him out the first time, he'd be fine today." Richard and I had taken that as a warning and told our boys that if they ever went to jail, our policy would be: "No bail." As young teens, the boys had agreed to our reasoning. But when we stuck with it later, Josh targeted all his anger at the most available target, which was, as usual, me. Richard had been out of town on business when Seth was arrested. Hearing about the arrest and being forced to make the decision long distance not to bail him out had been hard on Richard. During the next five days of Seth's imprisonment, Josh, who had not lived at home for about a year, had called me several times to curse at me for not bailing out Seth.

My sister Lois, a criminal prosecutor for thirteen years, said if Seth was not bailed out, then a public defender would be assigned to his case. Lois and my brother Paul both went to the jail to visit Seth, but I didn't—I was afraid of a response from him like Josh's. On the fifth day Seth called to say he'd be coming home because Josh had found a way to bail him out. Another bad decision.

When it came to raising my boys, I had wondered perhaps a million times, *What were they thinking?* After one difficult time, as I talked on the telephone with a friend who was raising nine boys, six of her own and three adopted into the family, I had moaned, "Karen, how do you know what these boys are thinking?" Quick as a flash, she had responded, "Oh! Boys don't think!" There was my answer. The day Seth walked out of jail just a few hours shy of having a free public defender, I knew what was going on. I had long since stopped asking what they were thinking. They weren't.

What Is Your Vision?

Seth's call saying he had bailed out had added another dilemma. Our house rules stated that if you lived at home, you couldn't do drugs. Sort of a no-brainer for parents, but unreasonable to my sons. I didn't know where Josh found the bail money unless it was from their drug-dealer friends, and with Richard out of town, I was frightened that some thugs might come to my house to get a payback. It sounds unreasonable to me now, but at the time I succumbed to fear. When Seth came home from jail, I told him he'd broken one of the rules of the house and that he'd have to live somewhere else. Wicked stepmother, right?

Richard supported my decision, but it left Seth in a terrible place. Seth had a felony arrest, no place to live, no job, no friends he could afford to hang around with because another bust would mean certain prison time, and now he couldn't have a public defender. So what does a young man do? About a month after Josh had bailed Seth out of jail, Josh called me at work and asked, "Do you know where Seth is?"

"Josh, what are you talking about?" My temper flared up. I had been tense before Josh called, worried about what was going to happen with Seth's life. Despite all we'd been through, I had invested years of my life into his, and I was having a hard time accepting him becoming a criminal.

"I don't know where he is. I think he might have gone to Mexico," Josh told me.

"Josh, you bailed him out. You took responsibility for him. HAVE YOU LOST YOUR BROTHER?" I screamed into the phone.

Days later, through Seth's and Josh's friends we learned that Seth had gone to Mexico and returned. His arraignment had been postponed, so he was still able to go to court and plead his case without serving jail time for bail-jumping or contempt of court. A few more months passed before I received a call from Seth.

21

"Mom, can I come home and live, just until my trial date?"

"What are you doing about your arrest?"

"I've found a lawyer, and I have a job, so if I live at home I can afford to go to court." Long pause. "I'll live by the rules. I understand them."

"I'll talk to Dad. Where can I reach you?"

"I'll have to call you again. I don't have a place to live right now."

It was one of the most heart-wrenching conversations of my life. My boy! He'd brought it on himself, yet it hurt to watch him live through the consequences of his choices. After we talked it through, Richard and I welcomed Seth back into our home. Richard had gone over the rules with him again, then we did all we could to make him feel comfortable and accepted.

This is called the "revolving door" syndrome, which is a pretty difficult subject. Is it right to welcome children back? Or is a decision a decision, and they just have to learn to live with it? And, if a parent welcomes them back, how many times can you allow them to break the rules again, be kicked out, only to return to break the rules yet again? Seth and I agree today that because Richard and I stuck by the rules, while allowing the children to return to try again to live up to the rules, we provided a fair environment and a challenge for Josh and him. For our family, this worked.

Waiting outside the courtroom for the hearing, I paced up and down the long hallway several times, keeping an eye on Richard, Seth and the lawyer. Their heads bobbed as they huddled in a little knot. My thoughts brought me up to the present, and curiosity drew me to them. I approached and heard the lawyer pleading with Seth to accept a plea bargain, spend a year in the penitentiary and not go through with the trial. He said the district attorney was out for blood and that Seth had drawn a very difficult judge. Seth would receive at least three years in jail if he went through with the hearing.

"What do you think?" Richard asked, straightening up to look at me.

"I think if Seth has decided to throw himself on the mercy of the court, he should," I said. "He's had enough time to think and pray about it. If he's comfortable with it, I'm behind him."

Seth had come back to live with us while awaiting this trial date, and Richard and I had watched him go through a roller coaster of emotions, almost always inching toward a new level of maturity. He had learned new habit patterns of holding a job, obeying the rules at home and working toward a goal. The Seth huddling with his lawyer was far different from the Seth who had been arrested, and I wanted to encourage his growth by backing him in what was perhaps his first mature, adult decision.

"I may need one of you to testify," the lawyer said, looking at Richard and glancing up at me. "Are you up to that?" We both nodded. As we began to file into the courtroom, I rushed down the hallway and called my mother and sister to ask them to pray. I'd never even thought about telling anyone where we were. Looking back on it, only my lawyer sister and Seth realized how high the stakes were that day. It might be a long time before Seth would join us at family dinner again. For whatever reason, that hadn't occurred to me.

We entered the courtroom and sat talking until we were called to our feet when the judge entered. In an instant the trial was in motion, and the next thing I knew, I was standing at the witness box with my hand raised and my stomach turning flips.

"Do you swear to tell truth, the whole truth and nothing but the truth, so help you God?" the judge asked me.

"Yes," I said, as I held his stare. He was a handsome black man with freckles and terrific frames for his glasses. He reminded me of a distinguished New York pastor with whom I was good friends. That thought relaxed me a little as I took my seat in the witness box. I was the first witness called, and I had no idea I'd be the only witness called.

"Mrs. Webster, why do believe your son should be let off from this felony charge?" Seth's lawyer asked. I was a little surprised that he asked such a gutsy question when he'd just met me, but I had an immediate answer for him. In the back of my mind, I may have wondered what was best for Seth, but on that witness stand I wanted to fight for his freedom.

"He was arrested only two weeks after his eighteenth birthday. Now he'll never get to vote because of those two weeks, never be able to rent an apartment or get a job without disclosing his felony record. It's going to affect his life forever because of fourteen days."

That was it—one question. He turned the questioning over to the district attorney, a woman perhaps a little younger than I with shoulder-length dark hair. She had an assistant at her side who pored over a stack of paperwork the whole time I was being questioned. I couldn't tell if they were preparing for their next case or if they'd come unprepared for this one. The district attorney opened her mouth and sounded just like my sister Lois when she picked a fight with me. Growing up with someone destined to be a lawyer wasn't easy, but it prepared me for this. Now I was calm. This was like talking to Lois.

"Mrs. Webster, do you even know what your son was doing that night?" she asked me. She had a sarcastic tone to her voice, just like Lois. And her question had been preceded by what seemed like a ten-minute tirade about how horrid my stepson was. I sat forward a little in my chair.

"No, I can't say that I do know what he was doing," I said. She looked at the judge and rolled her eyes. Just like Lois. I kept talking.

"Actually, my husband and I always taught our sons that

24

choices have consequences, that you are free to make the choice, but once made, you become the servant to that choice. We didn't hire a lawyer or bail him out of jail. He's done all that himself because he knew that if he got into it, it was up to him to get himself out. Now that you mention it, Seth and I have never sat down and talked about that night. He's his own man, and if he chooses to tell me about it one day, that's OK, but meanwhile it's none of my business."

She asked three questions, and I used each question to give the judge as much positive information about Seth and our family as possible. She stopped, with the smirk on her face slightly faded.

"Now, Mrs. Webster," the judge said looking down at me from his box about a foot above mine, "I'm confused. You said that Seth lives with you and his father, but used to live with his mother. Who are you?"

"I'm his stepmother," I answered, "and we've had custody of Seth and his brother for six years. We came to this courthouse right here to get them." I proceeded to give him some of our history of what the boys had been through.

"And why do you think this boy should be sent out in society again after what he's done?" he asked.

"Because he's a wonderful kid who did something wrong," I said. I looked at Seth and saw red rims around his eyes, something rare, since I'd seen him cry only twice in all those years. "He's talented, can pick up any musical instrument and start playing it. He's smart, took all honors classes before he dropped out of school. He's artistic, able to draw anything, and I'm sure he has a great future ahead of him in the field of art. He's athletic, funny, well-liked, social. He's just a great kid, but he's a little screwed up."

"And how'd he get that way?"

"He was pretty much that way when we got him."

SETH— "Your Honor, I call to the stand, in Mr. Seth Webster's defense, Joann Webster."

So there it was, the ultimate irony. The one person on whom I blamed all my problems. The one person I believed was out to ruin my life. The person I least expected ever to trust, taking the stand in my defense, stepping between my freedom and a five-year sentence. The "mean and wicked stepmother."

I felt my heart jump into my throat when I heard my stepmom's name called. There was so much tension between us. It seemed she was always on my case, making me feel as if I couldn't meet the high standards her family always set. For such a long time I couldn't get along with her. To me, we were always fighting about something. It seemed she always had at least one thing to be upset about, that no matter what I did, I was always screwing up.

Growing up with her seemed like such a hassle. If I wasn't doing one thing wrong then there was another. I felt like she was trying to make my life horrible on purpose. I had my own agenda, and this woman whom my dad married thought she had a say in it.

Later I decided it was easier to get along with her if I avoided her. I had never expected or wanted her to be involved in my life. I didn't trust her, yet now here she was taking the stand for my biggest screwup yet. How much more involved can someone be? I knew I had brought this all on myself, and I deserved what I got, but now things looked real bad. Here was her chance to let me know just how bad I had been.

Nine months earlier I had sat in jail for five days and figured out that I needed to accept the consequences of my drug bust. I was allowed one phone call a day, and on that fifth day I used it to page my friend Bryan to get word to my brother, Josh, not to bail me out. Josh didn't get the message and bailed me out anyway. I signed the forms saying I waived the right to a public defender, meaning that I had to show up for court with a lawyer I had to pay for myself. I had only ten working days to get a lawyer. I knew it was a big mistake. But once I did it, there was no going back. I didn't even have a job.

On the way home from the local jail, I figured up that I owed a bail bondsman and the court about a thousand bucks. Plus, I had to pay at least half a lawyer's fee for him even to show up at court.

The irony of it all was that I had lost the enjoyment of getting high. I was stuck in a cycle of having to sell drugs to support my lifestyle. While I was trying to think of ways to get out of this cycle, the last thing I ever expected to happen, happened—the consequence. I arrived at my parent's house where I had been staying. My stepmom opened the door just enough to see it was me, then told me as I stood on the porch, "You can't stay here. I don't know who's going to come looking for what, and I don't feel safe having you in the house. When Dad gets home, you can talk to him about it."

At this point, normally I would have taken out all my anger and frustration on her. "What the !#@%? You mean you're not letting me in the house? I've spent the last six days in jail without a change of clothes or a toothbrush. All I want is to take a shower and get cleaned up! Let me in!"

However, that day wasn't typical. Strangely enough I was beginning to understand why she did what she did, and I didn't even get mad about it. Somehow, for the first time I knew that what was happening was my own fault.

My grandpa says, "Everything in life works according to a pattern, based on a principle." When I heard that as a boy, it didn't make sense. Only after my arrest did I start to understand that actions have consequences. Once you put something in motion, something else will happen as a result. And I have the ability to choose what I put into motion—either good or bad.

I grew up with a warped perspective of life that I would have to understand before I could learn the truth about reality. I had never been taught how to mature. I just grew up any way I knew how. I used to think that when something happened, that was just the way it was. For all I knew, every situation was isolated from any other.

I always felt like I was a slave to whatever was going on. I didn't command situations. I wasn't in control of them. I was so intent on being a victim, I never considered I had control. I thought I just had to deal with situations as they happened. It never occurred to me that I was doing the same thing over and over again, and getting the same results.

My favorite saying was, "It's not my fault!" I said it so often that when we first went to live with my dad, he and I had a T-shirt made at the mall with my name and those words printed on it. For Josh, we got one that said, "It's not fair!" Though the shirts were a family joke, Josh believed the world was unfair to him, and I believed things were not my fault.

I always felt justified in everything I did because I believed every situation called for whatever reaction I had. It wasn't my fault how I reacted because, after all, I had no control over anything anyway. I felt powerless. At home, at school, even in the custody battle with the judge I felt dependent on others, with no real say in my own life.

People always told me I had potential. But potential was an abstract concept that didn't mean anything to me. I never understood that I was responsible for my talents and abilities, so I took them for granted.

Once, when I was thirteen, my stepmom invited this guy Franklin over to dinner whom she had met when he volunteered as a graphic artist for the Christian ministry where she worked. He was well-dressed, had wavy black hair and kept us laughing through dinner with his corny jokes. *Ba-ta-bing!* he'd say at the end of each joke. I felt comfortable around him.

What Is Your Vision?

When I learned that he was a successful graphic artist with his own agency, I showed him one of my drawings. I liked him when he complimented me on it and told me I had the talent to make it. I found out from my stepmom that he made money doing art, and I loved art, so I knew I could make money doing what I loved.

For some people, that would have been a life-changing moment. But I couldn't believe that about myself, so instead I got all wrapped up in my friends and their self-pleasing lifestyles. That night with Franklin turned out to be a fleeting revelation that I never thought about again until years later. I wasn't attracted to the things that were beneficial for me. These types of "moments" never stuck with me. However, I was always thinking about destructive things and found pleasure in chaos and disorder.

In all those years, I always thought I'd be an artist some day. I just didn't know how to make myself an artist. I figured it would just sort of happen to me—that's how things always worked—and, after all, the potential was there. It was a harsh reality when I was arrested. After a few days in jail I realized that things don't just happen, but I make things happen. Until then I had lived my life day-to-day. I never related what was going on one day with what went on the day before or with what would happen the next day. But I was figuring out there was a real chain of events and consequences for my actions.

By the time I was arrested, I had done so much wrong that I was proud of the "bad guy" status I'd achieved because it impressed my friends. However, first in jail and then on the day of my trial, reality started to set in. I realized that I wasn't the coolest kid in town. I wasn't the funniest. I wasn't the best I could be. I wasn't what my teachers, family and parents told me I was capable of becoming. Instead, for a fairly bright and talented kid, I ended up ashamed, alone, homeless, on trial for a felony arrest and needing money badly.

Under the circumstances, I had done what any person would

have done, if that person were Billy the Kid. I ran away to Mexico. It just so happened that after my release from jail, some friends of mine were making a run to Mexico to pick up some drugs. We all knew that I needed money and could speak Spanish, so it made absolute sense for me to go. The only thing wrong with this situation was that I wasn't even supposed to leave the county, let alone the state or country. Being at the end of my rope with nothing left to hold on to, I decided that the best thing would be to make it to Mexico and not come back.

We were there five days, getting high with the border patrol officers (on the Mexican side), downing bottles of clear tequila and Dos Equis beer and getting into a bar fight. Somewhere in there, I decided that being an outlaw wasn't the best decision after all.

I knew I had missed my arraignment and that the only thing left for me to do was to return to the United States and turn myself in. By God's grace, I found out that during my time in Mexico, the overbooked courts had postponed my arraignment and said they would notify me when it would be rescheduled, which would be no sooner than three months. Amazing. That's when I approached my parents asking for help.

I stood in court that day looking at the situation, trying to analyze what it all meant. I'd done a lot of drugs as my life wasted away to this point, and now I was trying to figure out what the reality was. This wasn't just a bad acid trip, but something real, something that would affect my life for a long time. They say certain moments are "sobering." For me, that was the literal truth.

I looked around the courtroom trying to grasp it all. There was my lawyer, a young guy making a buck, acting like all he cared about was getting me off the hook when he was dreaming about the Porsche I was helping him to buy. The assistant district attorney had one priority that day—to put me in jail for a long time. The judge had the final decision whether I had the right to continue living in society or had forfeited that right by choosing to live like an animal who had to be locked in a cage. At that moment I realized that none of these people knew me. None had ever seen my potential. They had seen hundreds of guys like me in the same situation. So what was different about me? Why did I think I should be treated any differently from other criminals who were locked up for less than what I had done?

My palms felt sweaty. I could feel my throat tightening. My eyes began to water as I realized, *There is no difference!*

If I was going to be put in prison, I deserved it. I had chosen to become a criminal. That's the scariest thing I have ever had to face.

Then came my stepmom, taking the stand in my defense. I didn't realize it then, but it wasn't just me who was on trial that day. It was our family. Even more so, it was my stepmom. This woman defending this young man as if he were her own flesh and blood also had to defend her own stepparenting. She had to justify to complete strangers the way she raised me, the influence she had on my life and the type of parent she had become. She had to convince them that she and my dad had taught me to be a responsible citizen and that if they would just give me a second chance, that's what I'd become. But I was so far from that! And I knew that she knew it.

My stepmom could have let me crash and burn. She could have refused to defend me on the stand. That's what I deserved. But to my stepmom's credit, she didn't let our past hinder our future.

2

MERGING VALUES

JOANN— Hollywood strikes again. Even though more than half the nation's population is involved in blended families, movies and television programs continue depicting stepfamilies with one basic problem: getting the child to like the stepparent. The typical fictional story ends with the stepparent and child reaching a new appreciation for each other and enjoying some activity together. The final scene fades out with the assumption that everyone lived happily ever after. Well, wouldn't that be nice?

Such images create two misunderstandings. First, it puts an unfair burden on stepparents to perform in a way that is satisfactory to a child, which also gives an unhealthy power to the child. Second, it gives the illusion that getting along together in a social sense is the answer to living together as a family. That's like saying that since you did so well dating, your marriage will be a breeze. Having fun is a necessary component of most relationships, and having fun makes the icky parts of life tolerable, but <u>learning how</u> <u>to have fun together is no solution in itself.</u> Many more issues must be resolved to create a happy blended family.

I remember discovering this secret after one painful family counseling session close to a year after Josh and Seth came to live with us. With the help of a counselor who specialized in adolescent behavior, we were uncovering the boys' hostilities toward parents and authority-figures in general. We learned in this session that they felt safe acting out their hostility toward their resident stepparent—which would be me. Oops, the hour was over. We filed out the door. The counselor, Richard and the boys seemed happy about the progress we'd made, but I was devastated. Since we'd driven two cars, Richard took the boys with him. I felt relieved to be left alone for the drive home.

So that's the way it will be? I wondered in a bit of a daze. *The boys will act hostile toward me, and everyone is just fine with that?*

As I walked through my front door, the telephone was ringing. On two occasions during the roller-coaster "blending" years, I received what seemed like a call from God—and this was one of them. My friend Honey from Tulsa was calling to chat and to say she'd been praying for me. I told her about the counseling session, and she said, "Joann, I feel God is telling me that you have a host of angels dispatched to help you and that you've been chosen for a job that no one else could do." She prayed for me, and we hung up.

I'll get back to those angels and that hostility—and that insensitive counselor—but the first thing her words planted in my mind was that I was in this situation to accomplish a specific purpose in the boys' lives. This meant that I was just like any parent with a destiny to fulfill, which was wrapped up in theirs. And this destiny would be unlocked according to God's will. *We were not thrown together at random, but I was me, and they were them, and God had a plan.*

What a different desire this understanding spurred in my heart compared with just wanting them to like me. The popularity contest was over. It was time to get serious about what God wanted me to do.

I didn't realize it then, but I took a huge step that day, one that would serve me well through all the upheavals to come. The bottom line was, no matter what anyone else thought or what society said, I was needed. God had put me in this situation for a purpose, and my job was to find and fulfill that purpose. It didn't matter if they liked me or if I liked them. This had more to do with God and me than with them and me. For a stepparent, that's a liberating and exciting revelation.

Children Are "Nations"

Abraham and Sarah made a few blunders, but what they did right, they did so right that millions of people throughout history have tried to follow their example to the present day. One thing Abraham and Sarah determined was that their children were "nations." They believed that by birthing and raising children, they were birthing and shaping nations.

By *nation,* the Bible means "a people." In the labyrinth of biblical types and shadows, "nations" or "lands" can pretty much be interchanged with "peoples" and "families." All of us who are parents are aware to some degree that our children will one day have families of their own and that their lives will intersect with countless others. Depending on how extra good or extra bad they are, our children could affect millions of people or even change history. We know this even if we don't think it or say it in quite that way. But can we imagine that our children are leaders of their own developing "nations"?

We've each created a "nation" in our homes with our own set of beliefs, rituals and, often, language. We have certain customs at birthdays and holidays. We give certain privileges at stages of a child's life. We go to bed each night in a certain manner. We even speak to one another using terms that only our families would understand. For example, my parents and siblings could say "peanut butter sandwiches" to each other, and it meant over-working ourselves. One of my nieces and I can say "spaghetti," and we'll burst into laughter. Families use language to develop something that is often like a secret code of communication, and very difficult for outsiders to penetrate.

Children have talents, traits and values—both inborn and acquired—that differ from others within the same family. Children carve their own nations out of the nation that is their family. They create something like subcultures within their family's culture. If they don't speak the same language, or if they choose to adopt different customs, the rub begins. As children draw closer to their teens and want room to expand their nations, this can become almost unbearable, even in nuclear families.

Sometimes a child's subculture is different and annoying, but we have to determine if it is "wrong" and cannot be tolerated under our roof. Traits may be as innocent as a love for horses or a habit of reading magazines, or as irritating as being a night person when everyone else needs to get up in the morning or being so social that the telephone rings nonstop. Some of this requires discipline, which we'll cover later, but some of this is an inborn trait or talent, which that child feels compelled to develop. By recognizing that children have their own strengths and desires, which are not always like ours, parents can keep from bogging down in useless debates and unnecessary irritations.

When Josh and Seth lived as adults with Richard and me, it was obvious we each had developed different rules for our lives. In my "nation," I can have a messy desk, as long as the rest of the house is clean. In Josh's "nation," the refrigerator, cupboards and even

35

the spice rack must be full. In Richard's "nation," you can never leave the house in clothes that have not been pressed. Seth's "nation" is full of car parts, computer parts, stereo parts, telephone parts, all of which are important to him—even if they're not useful to anyone else.

What seem like trivial traits reflect individual value systems within the larger family values we've merged. Our individual values can become so important to us that if the rest of the family doesn't recognize their significance it creates tremendous tension. We had to recognize that I wanted beds made even behind doors that are closed. Josh wanted to know the spice he needed was always there. Richard didn't want us using up his spray starch. And we had better not mess with Seth's computer.

It seemed easier to deal with my stepchildren when I recognized that, even as children, I needed to respect their autonomy as a nation, accept "cultural" differences and choose the way in which I would influence them. This was much easier than trying to force them to live my way, obey my rules and become the people I thought they should become. Respect is a necessary ingredient of true love. Stepchildren may or may not one day love a stepparent, but if the stepparent doesn't respect them, that day will never come.

Jesus said to take the gospel message to every "nation," and if we believe as Abraham and Sarah believed, this starts at home. The old adage says, "A man can win the world and lose his own family." Our family represents nations, so we start with them.

Impacting a Nation

It is a tremendous privilege for us to be given a task as a parent, stepparent, teacher, coach, pastor, caregiver or even neighbor to leave a positive, lasting impact to some degree on a young life entrusted to our care. It is awesome that God gives us the power to determine our *own* lives. The fact He trusts us with the life of a child can be almost overwhelming.

Yet to influence the child of a blended family, both biological parents and stepparents have subtle and obvious obstacles to overcome. The expectations of the biological parent on the stepparent can cause tremendous grief in a marriage, so the stepparent's obstacles need to be understood by both. Inheriting someone else's children is much like being given a jigsaw puzzle without a picture to go by and being expected to put it together.

One big obstacle for the stepparent is that they weren't around when this child, this "nation," was first being formed. They had no incubation stage to dream of a future for this child and perhaps pray over his or her destiny. Stepparents inherit an infant nation and are expected to nurture it, when they don't understand what it's all about. In a loony look at history, this would be like "step-citizens"— who weren't signers of the Declaration of Independence–being expected to lead the American Revolution and win–then being sent the bill for the war. Stepparents aren't imagining the same future for a child that the biological parent already sees. And, the biological parent often can't see the present situation as the stepparent sees it.

Another obstacle is that stepparents and stepchildren have no natural bond. For stepparents who take on an older child, they never see the child undressed. That may sound perverted in today's society, but a certain intimacy develops when a child is dependent upon someone at an early age. Not that getting children early ensures intimacy, because often younger children feel abandoned and rejected by a biological parent, which causes other problems. But having them early does promote a sense of mutual "knowing" that is harder to accomplish with older children.

Stepparents also don't name the child. Naming someone or something infers a right of possession. To name a child, or have someone's child named after you, has an unspoken proprietorship that comes with it. As Juliet discovered when she asked, "What's in a name?" the answer is, plenty! Sometimes a child's name can become a rub, in and of itself. I have friends whose son prefers to be called "John Junior" even though no "John Senior" is in sight. This cannot help but produce distance between the child and resident stepfather. A stepmother who would never in a zillion years have named a child after a character from the old TV series *Bewitched* raised another Samantha. These are often imperceptible, yet deeply felt stop signs that keep stepparents from feeling like they want to—or have the right to—"step in" and touch a child's life.

And it matters that stepparents did not contribute to the gene pool of the child. One of the thrills of child-rearing is to see a child do something you used to do, or still do—seeing facial expressions, talents or habits rise to the surface as the child grows. Fathers in general tend to relate to their children's achievements more than mothers, who tend to relate to their children's struggles. Stepparents will generally receive satisfaction only years after a blended family forms, and only if the child picks something up from that stepparent. That delay is often hurtful and sometimes fatal to the stepparent, because it is so easy for a stepparent to give up, thinking it's impossible to make an impression.

The child's genes create another problem for both parent and stepparent alike, in that often the child looks or behaves like someone whom parents, at best, have mixed feelings about—the Other Parent. Sometimes because of a parent's outright hostility toward the ex-spouse, he or she can throw the child into a quandary by insisting the child not behave in that way. The child is left feeling like part of him or her is evil.

Then there is the obvious outward behavior of the child, with which every blended family deals. The son who glares at the stepfather as he hugs his mother. The stepdaughter who jumps into the front seat next to her father, even though the stepmother is going to ride in the same car. The stepson who mocks his mother, just to see his stepfather's temper rise, so his mother can then defend him. On and on this junk can go if we allow it.

Values

The biggest obstacle of all for spouses, parents and stepparents is sharing values. What traits a child incorporates into his "nation"—what he likes or dislikes, wants to do or avoids, chooses to develop or squelch—is based on the intricate value system that child has developed. A differing value system draws a line of separation between family members deeper than anything else. A shared value system, more than anything else, will bring a family together.

Studies have identified three cycles in stepfamily life. First are high stress, disillusionment, conflict and division during the first two years. This is the period during which more than half of all stepfamily marriages fail. Because they don't see it as a phase, but as a fact, spouses tend to bail out before they've had time to blend. The second cycle is happiness, from the second to the fifth year. And third, if the children are entering adolescence around then, is a brief return to chaos. Going in reverse, the third, or "chaos," stage can be lived through with a healthy dose of respect and recognition of differences. It is not as fatal as the first. The second stage—who cares? It's a happy one.

The chaos stage, which lasts close to two years, I am convinced does not come from trying to organize bathroom time or determining how much salt everyone likes in the soup—it comes from merging *values.*

Values don't have to be good or bad; just being different will create stress. I learned about one family whose first major conflict came because the mother and her five sons had learned to value humor. In their interaction, they didn't reward each other just for

39

being *funny* but for being *sarcastic*. The more sarcastic you were, the more your family laughed, and the more rewarded you felt.

The boys' mom married a man who placed a huge value on patriotism. One of his and his daughters' favorite holidays was the Fourth of July when they studied and celebrated American Independence. He was gleeful about sharing this experience with his new wife and sons. In his mind, this was a tremendous opportunity for them to bond as a family.

Seated at the head of a table laden with an elaborate meal that was trimmed in red, white and blue decorations, the father launched into his Independence Day exercises. He asked each one at the table to tell what independence meant to them. No one volunteered to start, so he broke the ice and said he would start.

Midway through his discourse on independence, one of the five brothers started humming "America the Beautiful." The other boys heard it and started snickering, and soon tears were rolling down their mother's face as she, too, tried to squelch her laughter. The mother and her boys couldn't hold back, even though the father and his daughters were mortified and furious.

How each one felt about this might have amazed the others. The father was angry that he was disrespected, and his daughters were angry on behalf of their father. The stepmother realized the boys were rude to laugh when their stepfather was serious, but all he had to do was lighten up a little. The boys felt they were just being funny, which had always held the highest value.

Depending on your own values, you might have a different opinion. Rudeness aside, patriotism and humor are not opposites. In a nuclear family, the couple would have already established the rank of importance between these values and passed it on to their children. If this were *any* group of people who had worked or lived together for a period of time, they would have known that their sarcastic humor was OK, but if old Charlie wanted to talk patriotism, that value superseded sarcasm, and they had better be quiet while he talked. These kinds of values, and ranking of values, are only learned through experience.

No way exists to identify and delineate your value system before it collides with another, because it is too complex. The most you can hope for is respect and understanding all the way around, but even then, you may not understand how others feel before you've already hurt their feelings. Even if you tried to talk it all out until two o'clock in the morning—which is how boyfriends, girlfriends and newlyweds merge—for everything you remembered to warn the other person about or talk to the children about, something else still would pop up.

Building family walls of shared values and expectations requires stacking bricks of patience, respect, communication and understanding and holding them in place with the thick mortar of love and commitment.

Receiving custody of my children at ages twelve and fourteen, their values seemed set in concrete and in no way resembled mine. I was so idealistic, I didn't even realize how different we could be. Another pitfall of the "romantic" is they tend not to listen to anything they don't want to hear, and don't talk about their assumptions for family life because they believe everyone shares those assumptions. After all, didn't we all watch reruns of *Leave It to Beaver* and learn the same values?

Statistics were also against me. Men with no children of their own have the easiest time adjusting to stepfamily life. Women with no children of their own have the most difficult time. If all that were not enough, Dr. Bray's study found children in a new stepfamily may temporarily slip back into a younger developmental stage.[1]

Also, the stress of the first cycle of stepfamily life causes us to miss or misread signals from children and spouses alike. We're so busy putting out internal fires that we can't see an SOS sent from a troubled child. And we're so keyed up that instead of talking things through with a spouse, we tend toward faultfinding, yelling things like: "You were wrong to let those boys laugh!" "It's your fault for trying to be serious!"

Often in my family we hurt each other's feelings without knowing it. We had to keep hanging in with each other until our personal values began to emerge, and then merge together to form our core family values.

Our "False Start"

The first time we went to court as a family, I wore my pearls and tried to look like a middle-class wife from the sitcoms, just as I did at Seth's trial. We were fighting for custody, and we had to prove to a judge that we had what it takes to form a family. Again, I seemed to be the one on trial. People seem to take this mean-and-wicked-stepmother thing seriously!

Feeling very housewifey in my floral dress and permed brunette hair, I entered a tiny side room between the courtroom and the judge's actual office. A chair was pulled up to the side of an old dark wood table, where a robust man was seated, about the same age as the table. Our lawyer made a quick introduction then left me on my own.

Richard and the boys were waiting in the shiny paneled hallways of the historic old courthouse in Fort Worth. It seemed odd that they were the ones with everything riding on the judge's decision, yet I was the only one called into the judge's chambers.

"Do you really want these children?" the judge asked. He had the face of a grandfather and appeared to be as concerned for me as he was for the boys. "You know there is a lot of responsibility in taking on children."

I explained that Richard and I had already counted emotional, physical and financial costs, going over our budget to figure out how we could afford two growing boys with all the clothes, activities and mountains of food we were aware that they could consume.

The judge studied me, looking past every answer at my eyes, my face, my gestures. This was a man schooled in sizing people up, examining every nuance to determine character. I became somewhat nervous under his gaze, and babbled on about helping with homework, securing tutoring where necessary and trying to rebuild anything that may have been damaged within them. Having degrees as Richard and I had, and with Richard's experience at working in a troubled-boys home and psychiatric ward, we may have appeared more prepared than most parents, and I suppose my sincerity helped.

On the other hand, thinking about the strikes against us, it was miraculous that we were granted a custody hearing at all. I wasn't a mother! I was a devoted aunt and had worked with children in churches, but there's nothing like motherhood. Not only that, Richard had been in the military and missed huge segments of the boys' developing years. It is not unusual for otherwise devoted fathers to disappear after divorce, becoming more of an "Uncle Daddy." For Richard, as for many, remarriage had afforded him the opportunity to reconnect with his sons.

Moreover, the kids and the Other Parents were residents of another state. Now we were asking to go from twice-a-year visitation to full-time custody, and the judge bought it, making the decision in our favor. Presto! Four strangers became a family. We later had to attend a trial that the boys' mother attended, and after that trial, the judge made a permanent decree, giving us her children. This was not a great way to develop a relationship with the ex-spouse.

In the divorce culture in which we live, people tend to be

nonchalant about families, as if we can form a family like the NBA draft forms a team. A center from here, two forwards from there, add some guards and you have a team. Not hardly. They still have to learn to play together. Yet our society perpetuates a myth that we can take one father here, one mother there and some children and leave it up to them to create something resembling a nuclear family. Not hardly.

In our case, the judge and I both knew something had to happen for those boys, but his experience made him more cautious while my idealism made me more hopeful. Hope won.

After the boys moved in, I found out what no one had told me. What no book said. What no one was able to tell me, perhaps, with my pie-in-the-sky, we-have-our-budget attitude about how organized and wonderful it would be. The truth was, I was prepared to help my children according to *my* view of life. I had prepared myself to sacrifice, to help them become what *I* thought they should be.

The first glimmer I had of reality came from Josh. He brought home his homework and told me he had a test the next day. I helped him study that night, keeping him away from the television downstairs while we drilled upstairs in his bedroom on the various answers. The result? He never had another test during his entire school career. At least not that he ever told me. They just didn't give tests at that school, as far as he was concerned.

His grades were all over the place. He struggled with his attention span so much that I took him to a local university for testing for ADD. I felt triumphant when the lead psychologist looked him in the eye and said, "Josh, you're intelligent enough to learn whatever you want to learn." For a kid who had been told he was stupid by authority figures, this was a huge moment, and great to witness. He didn't have ADD after all, but he did have deeply held beliefs about himself and the world. The only thing that school offered his value system was an opportunity for a social life. Academics were foreign to him. I had never imagined a kid would *want* to fail. This was not just against my values. It was far beyond my scope of understanding.

Seth was another story. He tested so high that he was put in all honors classes. The problem was that, like his brother, he could not have cared less about school. Night after night I worked with him on essays for Honors English and on memorizing stuff neither of us had ever heard of before for Texas history. Studying Texas history was like Chinese water torture, only without the water, just facts about Texas dripping on our heads and hard tests that had to be passed each week. The mention of that class today can still give us both headaches. Seth remembers the friends he met in the class and the fact that the word *Texas* derives from *Tejas.* Other than that, we're both a total blank.

Studying with the boys was a dismal failure in every respect. After a while, I happened onto the idea that they didn't *want* to do well in school. Their values were, among a few other things, to be popular, have girlfriends and get money. What is an ambitious parent to do with *that?* The only usefulness I could serve was for money, and we had precious little of that. We hadn't worked the lawyer bills into our budget, so we were more than just strapped. We were not making it. Something fired in my brain during those first months of school, and I realized that if I didn't find some common ground with these kids, our family was doomed.

Shared values define a family. They are part of what makes a family different from roommates. But what could we share? I liked literature, museums, a well-decorated and clean home, parties, good foods, foreign films, interesting friends. They liked video games, fighting, punk rock, MTV, getting in trouble, sleeping in late and leaving dirty clothes wherever they fell. We needed something.

CAN STEPFAMILIES BE DONE RIGHT?

CREATING SHARED VALUES

In order for the family to work, the first thing a parent has to value is the child. This doesn't mean the child is favored over the spouse—far from it—but that the child is shown that he or she matters in the newly forming family. From Miss Manners to the sharpest psychologist, everyone seems to agree that it is best for the children to be involved in the marriage ceremony when the blended family becomes an entity. This helps establish the child's place, which sets the stage for what is to come.

Just for that reason, Richard and I moved our wedding ceremony from Texas to California and married close to where the boys were living at the time so they could be part of it. It was our first terrific memory together, and I'm still glad we did it.

A child cannot be given power over parental decisions, but children can be given value by allowing them to have appropriate input in decisions. They can help to choose meals for the family or be filled in on the parents' decision to buy a new car or plan a vacation. Expressing interest also establishes a child's value. Listening to silly schoolyard stories, attending recitals and games, taking them out to lunch after a daytime orthodontist appointment, contacting the teacher about a grade—these tiny acts add up to a feeling that the child is wanted and important to the parent.

The parents themselves may not feel valued or appreciated. That's why parents are adults. We're supposed to be able to handle those emotions and continue sacrificing for the welfare of the family even without immediate rewards. I would not even venture to guess how many times I said to myself, *Somebody has to be the adult here.* I elected myself every time. I hate to admit that it wasn't natural.

As a stepmother, I occupied the low ground in my children's value system. The fact is, most stepchildren do not want another parent. My boys required a mother, and their biological mother, who was their first choice, lived far away. I was down the list, vying for a spot somewhere near Texas history.

I worked on valuing the children, but even that wasn't enough. Much of the time they didn't value themselves. Since they wouldn't even study for a test unless I studied with them, it was obvious they weren't as interested in sacrificing for their own welfare as I was. Assessing the situation, I made some good decisions that worked. One thing we all agreed on was that we adored Richard—well, during those tumultuous years this was sometimes true of them more than me. He was our common bond, so I worked with that.

One of the first defining moments of our new family was when we threw Richard a surprise birthday party. I suggested it to the boys, and they helped me plan with great enthusiasm. I decided to hold it at our house, only later realizing that meant I would have to take Richard away before the party and wouldn't be there when the thirty-plus friends I'd invited arrived.

While Richard was at the gym that morning, the boys and I cleaned and cleaned and cleaned together—even their bedrooms, because I said people would go there. Then we arranged some dirty laundry and dishes around the house so Richard wouldn't notice what we'd done. We also shopped together for party supplies and hid them in the garage. I asked a friend to bring decorations over after I left with Richard, and another to bring the cake. Then I went over a precise list of what the boys needed to do. They were thirteen and fourteen, and they knew I was entrusting them with a big job. That was good for us.

Later that evening, as Richard and I walked across the lawn toward the house, I didn't even care about what the boys might have done in our absence. I was going to have fun, regardless. But when the door flew open, there were all the people, the decorations, the cake, the boys—and everything was as perfect as could be imagined. People laughed that Josh tried to extort tips from them for parking their cars in a nearby church parking lot, but other than that, the kids were perfect, and the evening was a huge success. And people did use the boys' bedrooms to practice some skits we did, so I was even vindicated in my demands for total cleanliness.

When Richard and I rolled out of bed the next morning, I went to the top of the stairs and screamed for him to come look. The boys had gotten up early and cleaned the entire downstairs! The crepe paper was gone, the kitchen was clean, and they even had vacuumed. I provided fun for them and a way for them to feel good about themselves, and they responded by acting on my values and cleaning the house. What a triumph.

The next year, I knew enough to do something memorable again, but I didn't think they'd do well with a party two years in a row. Richard had been saying for months that he wanted a gray suit. I let the boys donate some of their allowance so they would feel equal and included in the surprise, and Josh and I went shopping while Seth kept Richard busy elsewhere. On the way home, Josh and I brainstormed about how to surprise Dad. We had picked up dry cleaning earlier, so Josh put the suit in with our dry cleaning and we left it in the car. At home, we all signed cards and Josh sneaked outside to stuff them in the suit's pockets.

The next morning, on Richard's actual birthday, we were all downstairs when I said, "Josh, I forgot the dry cleaning in the car."

"Oh, Mom!" he whined.

"Just do as your mother says, Josh," Richard commanded. The boys and I stole looks at each other because it was going just as we'd planned. Josh brought the suit inside and stood in the front hallway.

"Where'd you get that?" I asked.

48

"This is what you picked up," Josh said.

"Well I don't think that's Dad's."

This attracted Richard's attention and he went over to look at the "wrong" dry cleaning. His face turned pink and a nervous smile flickered. "This suit is just what I wanted. They must have given you the wrong clothes. I'll have to take it back."

"Try it on first," Seth suggested.

"Yeah, try it on," Josh said.

We could see a struggle on Richard's reddening face. The boys urged until he slipped on the coat.

"It fits perfect!" Seth said. "Hey—there's something in the pocket!"

Richard started pulling out the cards. "You guys…"

The boys told everyone about that morning. They were so proud of our family, so proud that we were fun and funny and enjoyed one another. Not only was it funny, it made an outstanding memory for us as separate entities to come together and experience the sweet satisfaction of giving the perfect gift to someone we all valued.

Now that I'd discovered how to hook into my boys' value system, I took more elaborate measures to connect in places of common interests. I once conducted a "finance seminar" with the boys, since they were interested in money and expensive cars. We sent out questionnaires to male adult friends asking how much education they had, what had contributed most to their success and if they felt satisfied that they had achieved their dreams. To a man, they all sent them back.

The next phase was to give the boys newspapers and ask them to find out the costs for what they thought was "bare minimum" existence, "average" living and then the "ultimate" lifestyle that was their dream. Their inflated ideas seemed to shock even them. They had no idea Ferraris and Lamborghinis were so expensive to buy or maintain. They didn't realize what monthly payments were required for the big houses in which some of their friends lived. The final phase involved learning how much various jobs paid. They were surprised to find that if they made only minimum wage, they wouldn't even be able to afford to live at what they considered "bare minimum."

The research became tiresome to them, so for our last session, I took them to an inexpensive dessert bar I knew about at a local Marriott. It was pretty quiet in the restaurant as businessmen sat around in meetings and waiters and waitresses spoke in hushed tones, hoping not to disturb any big deals in the making. Before we left, Josh eyed the wrapped candies in a decorative glass container in the middle of the table. "Mom, could I take some of that?" he asked.

Since I'd just tortured him through this finance seminar, I thought the least I could do was say yes. He stuffed his shirt pocket with the candy, then we stood up to leave. As we did, his pencil fell, and he stooped over to get it. The entire restaurant seemed to reverberate with the sound of a rock waterfall from those candies thundering to the floor out of his pocket as he bent over. Josh glanced up at me red-faced. Seth and I about choked, trying not to giggle as we helped pick up the candy. Then we all rushed into the cool night air and exploded with laughter.

The candy free-fall is all the boys remember about the "finance seminar." But learning how to invest in the market or create a family budget was not the point, even though it would have been nice for them to exercise financial responsibility at a young age. Instead, I was happy with the intangibles they gained. First, they learned that I was concerned about them and that grown men were also—enough to reveal some private life lessons. Second, they learned that money had value. Third, they learned that they needed to become concerned about making and spending money at some point in their lives. This was enough. The exercise paved the way for another shared value.

THE REWARDS

Building on these little, sometimes silly victories over the years, I ended up introducing the boys to everything I valued and opening doors for them to share with me what they were beginning to value. They both learned to enjoy museums, for example, maybe because talking about art made them sound "more mature" than their friends and provided them with opportunities to show off with teachers in front of the other kids. I put no pressure on them when we went. Other than asking them to keep their voices down, I didn't force them to like what I liked—just to show up.

One night we needed to go to downtown Dallas for something, so I asked if they'd mind going early and stopping by a special evening exhibit at the Dallas Museum of Art. We became separated in the crowd, and when I saw them again, it was across a sea of fancy people dressed in black with champagne flutes propped in their hands. I smiled to watch my teenagers standing in front of an abstract work, murmuring to each other with their hands cupped over their mouths and laughing. Even without expensive black clothes or champagne, they looked a cut above the rest of the crowd, like art critics who "got" the painting and were laughing "with" the artist. In reality, no doubt they were making fun of the artist or some naked body parts sticking out here and there.

Yet these were rewarding moments. They were like the time when Josh, in his late teens, was living away from home and called me to ask for directions to the local Shakespearean festival. Here he was asking for my help to do something I really, really liked even though we were miles apart in every other way. My heart soared.

Exchanging viewpoints and new experiences with each other

today is one of our greatest joys. Each time we have a good discussion, I get that terrific feeling as if I've won someone over to my point of view or taken someone to a place that is special to me, and they enjoyed it. That great feeling isn't because we agree on everything, but because we agree that we enjoy discussing things with each other. Those are the bonding moments we learned to share and value.

"Work on Yourself"

Every member of a blended family is wounded. Divorce or death has touched all, and each has responded in an individual way, adopting a unique pattern of healing or avoidance of pain. Time doesn't heal all wounds. Broken bones that are not set don't become reset and heal right just because of time. Instead, they harden into place until they cannot be reset. If we drive down a wrong street, time only takes us farther from our destination, not nearer. Time, plus the introduction of some healing elements, can heal, however. Once a healing element is introduced, then time can do its wonderful work.

It was by the grace of God that I came to understand my purpose and to see what was happening below the surface in my family. God didn't put me in that family to teach the boys a love for museums or parties or gift giving or financial stewardship. God put me in the family to administer His love and grace. God gave the world Jesus because He loved us, and He gave Jesus a mission to seek and to save. My pastor teaches, "The purpose of love is to save." God wanted to introduce my love into my boys' world to save them. I am sure of that today. But my love could not flow, and nothing I did would matter unless I took care of my own heart.

I had to stop worrying about whether or not the boys liked me and concentrate instead on whether God liked what I was doing. He promises in His Word that when our ways please Him, even our enemies will be at peace with us. My stepsons believed I was their enemy many times. They pitted their wills and their values against my will and my values. But as I pressed into God, I found ways to build thousands of tiny bridges over to the unhealthy land my sons occupied. In time, I was able to invade their land and take Jesus' love and healing with me.

My mother was without doubt the sweetest and most merciful person on earth. Perhaps once in her life I heard her give the directive "Work on yourself," yet it has echoed in my heart ever since. She said it in regard to women who complained about their husbands. Sometimes there is nothing you can do with a husband or family member who won't do right, act right or participate in the family right. But her point was, we can always do something with ourselves.

That's how I feel about being part of a blended family. Sometimes we face circumstances over which we have no control. Everyone does. Even driving down the freeway or standing in a grocery store line, we are at the mercy of others. But we can always control our own reactions and responses.

In our families, we can always enlarge our own hearts to accept others and help save them. We can step inside their shoes and see that they are living out what is in their hearts. We can validate and approve of those things that are at least somewhat wholesome, while being understanding and prayerful about what is unwholesome. We can also expose ourselves, risking rejection, to share something we value with others, in order to build a bridge to connect our minds and, perhaps later, our hearts.

The issue is how to get from here to there. My friends have a theory that children should be shrink-wrapped and placed in a time capsule from ages twelve to twenty. At times, it might also seem that if the Other Parents would just shrivel up, our problems would be solved. Yet children require going through developmental stages, and other sets of parents have a right to and might be good for the child's life, as hard as that is to admit for some people.

To span the gulf between where we are and where we want to be, we need to get over bad attitudes toward others, accept the situation we're in, adjust our expectations to our newfound reality and work harder on ourselves than we do on anyone else. If we work on ourselves, perhaps we'll be the first who heals, or the first who accepts and loves the other. Maybe the changes in us will cause a change in others. Even if they don't, at least we'll have something to show for the difficulties we went through.

I tell my friends when they go through difficulties: Change! Why go through agony if we don't end up with something to show for it in the end? Just about any situation, when given over to God, can produce lasting change for the good in our own lives. One of Dr. Bray's "tasks" for stepfamilies is "managing change."[2] Stepfamilies are chameleon-like, ever changing, flexible, dynamic rather than static. We have to be willing to change.

It's humbling yet necessary to admit that if problems exist in a family, and we are part of that family, then we are part of the problem. As right as we feel, as noble as we feel, and even if others are doing outright horrid things, there is always room to work on ourselves.

"Sticking it out" until the child turns eighteen is not an attitude that makes life worth living. What victory is there in tolerating something for a period of time? That's like boiling life down to a contest of who can hold their breath under water the longest. What does it matter? Holocaust survivor Corrie ten Boom once said to "live before an audience of One." If we make our ways pleasing to God and live as we would imagine Christ would live in our situation, then we can rest—rest!—in the knowledge that we've done all we can and that God will take it from there.

My children were "codependent" and had experienced a dysfunctional relationship with their stepfather, so I attacked that hurtful lifestyle by addressing it in myself as much as within them. The rules of a dysfunctional family are: "We don't talk. We don't feel. We don't trust." Dysfunctional families don't talk about the problems—the alcoholism, abuse, chronic lying. As a result, the children learn to numb themselves to it, and as a result of denying their own feelings, they learn not to trust anyone.

Fed up with my boys' behavior one day, I typed out on a bright green sheet, "Webster Rules: We talk; we feel; we trust; we love." I tried to live by those rules daily, and time became my friend. Changes did take place. No one else in the family even remembers that bright green paper on our refrigerator door, but it was a good reminder for me, something to which I could aspire. My hope was that if I worked on myself, did what I could and expanded my capacity for love, God would take it from there. My boys didn't believe in my love. If people don't believe in our love, they can't believe in our God. God had to intervene. We needed a miracle. And we got one.

SETH— I think most kids have the fantasy that they were adopted, but their real parents are going to come along at any minute, take them away to a beautiful home and lavish them with gifts. For a while, I thought my fantasy had come true. My brother and I had summer and Christmas visitation with my father and stepmother after they married. We were always excited to see them. One summer I wrote an essay on my dad's typewriter about visiting my dad and stepmom and called it "Six Weeks in Paradise."

Those type of fantasies always branch from some dislike the child has in his home. My dislikes were based on the fact that I was growing up in an abusive home. My stepfather and mother married shortly after my father and mother divorced. They had custody of both my brother and me and had a daughter of their own, my half-sister. I can't really understand or explain why my stepfather was so angry, but he was. His punishments were inconsistent and random at best. Although many bad things happened, the most potent memories I have are of the leather belt.

If my brother and I were in trouble, we would most often get beat with this sturdy, braided leather belt. Josh and I would have to take our pants down, and we would get spanked on our bare butts. It didn't leave me with an understanding of discipline—it left me with a feeling of shame and grief.

I hated watching my brother get spanked. The long minutes before my stepfather came in to administer the punishment were agony. I could see, even at that young age, the fear overwhelming my brother. My stepfather hated "wussies," so Josh would do his best to choke back his tears, with my support, so as not to upset my stepfather further.

Josh was always spanked first. Every time was the same. My stepfather would get ready to spank, and Josh would scream and jump in fear and anticipation of the pain. Every jump increased the number of spankings. Ten, fifteen, even twenty times that belt would come down. I would always be second. I was stubborn and refused to let my stepfather know how much pain he was inflicting. I would stand there like a brick wall. The only emotions I displayed were those of a statue, if it could cry silent tears. We would have purple and blue welts from our backs to our legs for the next couple of days, but the shame and embarrassment went deeper and lingered for years.

This is just one type, a more organized type, of the punishment we endured, but we always lived under this man's tyranny. We never knew what to expect next. We had some great times with my stepfather, but those memories are few and far between in comparison with the vivid memories I have of the pain in that home with him.

A number of problems came from growing up like that, but two stick out to me the most. First, my brother and I developed a co-dependent relationship that we had to battle for nearly a decade to overcome. He had a need to be needed, and I felt it was my obligation to do as he wished. He would often manipulate me, and I justified it, developing a need to be manipulated.

The second was the alienation from my family on my mom's side. Immediately after the custody battle, things changed. Josh and I were now viewed as jerks like my real father. That was pretty bad. I remember the words, "You're letting your father brainwash you."

To this day, it's not necessarily believed that we were abused as children, so the grounds on which the custody battle took place were invalid in their eyes. Things are getting back to normal as we've been able to put the past where it belongs for now—behind us. But for a number of years, my relationship with that side of the family was awkward, to say the least.

However, visiting my dad and stepmom was exactly what I thought I wanted. It was my fantasy come true. Since my stepmom's side of the family didn't get to see me year round, they made sure to make me feel at home and loved by giving me time, money, clothes—just about anything a kid could imagine.

I remember most the things we did—Six Flags, eating out at restaurants, camping, renting movies, just doing stuff. Everything we did was fun, and there wasn't a lot of time not doing anything. We hung out with the kids at church and with my cousins. We were always going to see someone or spending the night at someone's house. I remember getting hundred-dollar bills from my grandpa, too. He was part of that family to which I'd always fantasized I belonged. The ones who could give me lots of money, take me to cool places, buy me cool stuff.

At my regular home I didn't get to do those things all the time. I had to play with the same kids, do chores, never got any money, and there just wasn't as much fun. I came into this new family thinking that I would get to do what I wanted and be loved and appreciated for whatever that was.

The reality of the situation was something I never considered. It was opposite of the way I perceived it. For every McDonald's meal we ate, or Six Flags ticket they bought, my father and stepmom had put away what little money they could every month just for us to have during those six weeks. Everyone in the family saved up vacation time and days off to use around our visitation. I never understood that people were sacrificing so much of their time or money for me. They may have expected me to appreciate their sacrifices, but that was outside my range of understanding. I didn't.

I moved to Texas and instead of going to Six Flags every day, I had to start school, meet a new set of friends and fit in with a family that wasn't on vacation all the time. My dad and stepmom were strangers. Their parenting style was different from what I was used to. The value system was different. I no longer knew what was a priority and what wasn't.

I had spent my life perfecting a method of living in a certain atmosphere that no longer applied. I had developed a set of values that fit into my previous family. However, now those values were being challenged. Growing up as a latchkey kid in my other home meant that I spent a lot of time at friends' houses doing punk-kid things: R-rated movies, MTV, pornography and other influences shaped my thinking.

My stepmom came into our relationship with her own set of values and knew what she wanted to instill in me that would contribute to my character. But she was under the assumption that I would appreciate her helping to take me out of the old situation. I didn't. I was relieved to be in a better atmosphere, but I didn't want to change. I couldn't see any immediate worth in it. It was a long-term thing she was doing, but I based my life on instant gratification. If it didn't help me *right now,* I didn't want it.

We both came into our relationship with our own expectations. My stepmom believed that she would be able to impart culture and help me become a better person. I thought she should let me do whatever I wanted. Neither of us understood the other's perspectives. We rushed hand-in-hand to the doorway of our relationship and were shocked to find that upon entering, we took to opposite corners of the room.

I was used to being criticized for doing things wrong and couldn't see any difference with my stepmom's approach. The difference was that she wasn't just telling me what I was doing wrong, she was showing me how to do it right. No one had ever taught me how to do right before. I didn't know what constructive criticism was. I had a filter on my mind that only let through negative criticism, so without even listening, I figured she was telling me I was wrong. She became frustrated because I didn't value my own character. I became frustrated because I was annoyed by what she was trying to do, so I fought it.

My stepmom attempted to help me understand the value of what she was teaching me. For example, she thought that table manners were important. She would teach me what I needed to know and then take me into atmospheres that required good conduct. She hoped I would appreciate being able to fit in. But my negative filter was so thick that when we did go to a nice restaurant, I interpreted what she was doing as saying, "This shows I'm right and you're wrong."

On occasion, a light did burst into my eyes, and in those few moments I could see how her efforts *did* help me. Like when my brother wanted a formal sit-down dinner for his sixteenth birthday, and he and I had the best, or only, manners at the table.

It takes time for kids to understand the value of what any parent is trying to teach them. If a stepparent doesn't have an intimate relationship with a stepchild, then it is even harder for that child to appreciate the stepparent's values. Kids need time, consistency and clarity to come around and a clear understanding of the stepparent's reasons for what is happening.

If you're a stepchild and you don't like the way your stepparents are trying to involve themselves in your life, then talk to them. Ask them what they expect or want from you in a calm and adult manner. Try to listen well enough to hear what they hope you'll learn. Then let them know what you want and expect from yourself and them. You don't have to fight or throw a tantrum. Communicate.

Acceptance was what I valued most. I had an overall feeling of rejection that is inevitable for any child of divorce. Even though I was too young to understand it, and never felt that the divorce was my fault, I still felt rejected. Every relationship that failed in my life reinforced that feeling.

I wanted more than anything to be accepted by my friends. I didn't have an innate sense of respect for my dad and stepmom, and didn't seek their acceptance. For my friends, though, I felt that their acceptance was crucial. I began to do things I wouldn't have done before. My friends weren't making me do them. Peer pressure is rarely like that. Every parent wants to believe it's a child's awful friends who make him or her do things. But it was my friends and me together who wanted to experiment with what we knew was taboo. We all happened to agree on the excitement we got from trouble.

Rebellion was a full-fledged value for me. I felt oppressed growing up. There was no room for argument with my stepdad or for exercising my own opinion. I moved in with my dad and stepmom, and the oppression wasn't there. I had no fear in standing up and voicing my opinion. They welcomed hearing my side of things. Yet I couldn't distinguish the difference between having a difference of opinion on something that didn't matter with rebelling against something that did matter. And discipline didn't get my attention or even cause me to think twice about rebelling.

In Texas, the schools were stricter. I had to change classes for the first time and carry a different colored notebook to each class, which the kids had been doing for a year already, but was all new to me. I made friends with Ryan in band and with his brother Randy in science. Our science teacher, Mr. Cook, gave Randy and me lots of after-school detentions, because no matter what he did, we kept talking, even when he moved us across the room from each other. He later moved one of us to first period and one to sixth.

I had never done homework, which was a big deal to Miss Roundtree who taught Spanish and Texas history. In her Spanish class, I would get "zeros" and sit and talk to friends. Although my grades suffered, she was a good teacher, so I learned Spanish and speak it today, but I doubt that's a consolation to her or any other teacher for all I put them through. But homework became an issue for me. I discovered that my friends like Ryan and Randy who weren't in honors classes didn't have as much homework as I did, which didn't seem right. I felt I was once again a victim of injustice. I insisted my parents let me drop honors classes the next year.

My new school was also the biggest I'd ever attended. There hadn't been a "popular" kid when I was younger. Everyone did the same things, so there weren't cliques or "types." Now there was a "most popular kid in the school," and people were separated into band nerds, jocks, science and math geeks and other cliques. I desperately wanted to fit in. I started caring less about school and more about being cool. Maybe I was dealing with rejection and needed acceptance, but I didn't think about things like that at the time.

I became an angry, rebellious student. If the teachers made demands that angered me, I would argue that they could not tell me what to do. I had a negative overconfidence. I felt strong in the fact that I wasn't afraid of discipline. I'd had worse, and a little detention didn't faze me. I would butt up against authorities that should be respected. Anyone else would be scared to death being called into the principal's office. He didn't scare me. It was like all the other students had eight periods, but I had nine—the ninth was in the principal's office. I didn't value obedience because I didn't see any real problem with my rebellion.

My blatant rebellion was coupled with a love of being the center of attention. Being sarcastic and making fun of teachers, getting a teacher upset to make the kids laugh or making fun of a teacher behind his or her back to get the class laughing was important to me. I loved being able to get a rise out of people. The consequences for bad behavior never seemed bad enough to make me stop. The only problem with detention was that it was boring. I would always get extra days tacked on because I would talk in the detention hall. I didn't care.

3

BUILDING UNITY

JOANN— "Mom, I'm in love," Josh announced one day when I returned home from work.

"Wow," I said, as I stood in the kitchen in my heels, starting to cook dinner. "Who's the lucky girl?"

"I just met her. Her name's Michelle."

"Well, how do you know you love her when you don't really know her yet?"

"I *do* know her," he insisted. "Her name's Michelle."

Conversations like this always made me want to laugh, but I learned to laugh later and keep my boys talking whenever they were willing to talk. *Not* talking was always the bigger problem. In talking we might have problems, but if we communicated, we could always find a way to deal with them.

In a brilliant book titled *Traits of a Healthy Family,* researcher Delores Curran identified those traits. After studying responses from hundreds of family professionals, her research uncovered that of all the things a family did, learning to communicate was the most important of all. Trait #1 was, "The healthy family communicates and listens." Trait #13 was, "The healthy family fosters table time and conversation."[1] Without communication, the child's imagination and guesswork take over.

In a stepfamily, children can feel lost. They need to know someone in charge is thinking about their concerns. We might feel like the best parent on earth, getting up every day to go to work, paying the bills and keeping the refrigerator stocked. But if we don't *communicate* our concern, they won't get it.

Good communication leads to being known. Knowing and being known makes a family a family instead of just a group of roommates who react to one another but don't respond to one another's needs. If you don't know one another, you can't care about one another. Many parents don't seem to realize that their children want to talk, and that includes stepchildren. A taciturn eight-year-old who doesn't make a peep around the house might shock his stepfather when the dad observes him in the middle of a soccer game, yelling and shouting to his teammates. Why does the child feel like talking to them when he doesn't talk at home? Because communication includes both talking and listening.

Active listening is an art. Without it, we just wait for someone to stop speaking so it will be our turn to talk. One of the greatest compliments of my life came from a friend who had called with a problem. In the middle of the conversation, she interrupted herself and gushed, "You are the best listener I've ever known!" What she didn't know was that my stepsons had taught me how.

GETTING COMMUNICATION STARTED

Eloquence never comes from the mouth of the speaker, but from the ear of the hearer. I learned to listen without giving judgment and was dumbfounded at the things my children would tell me.

64

Sometimes it was everything I could do not to shut them up by saying, "You're not supposed to tell me that! Parents don't want to hear something like THAT!" My children had come into my home with values that differed from mine, so their stories sometimes dizzied my mind and jarred my sensibilities. But the only reason my family ever shared a single value was that we communicated. As I listened, invisible ties rushed through those words from their heart to mine. They appreciated me for listening, and when enough ties had been formed, they loved me for it.

When children talk, it's not time for parents to correct, judge their words, launch into a discourse or sermonize. It's a time to ask more and more about what they feel and to allow them the freedom to air it out. Feelings are important because emotions motivate us. More than any information children receive in school or at home, their emotions will move them to action. That's why taking drugs isn't as simple as "saying no." As my pastor says, "In order to say 'no,' you must have a deeper 'yes.'"

A talking child gives the parent an opportunity to validate his or her feelings, even if we disagree with the facts. Without disagreeing, we can question the child and, through our questions, lead him or her to answers we've already discovered. Motivational speaker Tom Hopkins has made a fortune teaching salespeople how to ask questions that lead potential clients to a purchase.[2] Far from being manipulative, this is a wonderful technique for enlightenment. Truths we ourselves discover sink in much deeper and last much longer than anything someone else says.

Let's say Seth tells me matter-of-factly, as he often did, that he wants to beat up a boy at school. I ask him why. He says it's because of what the boy said. I ask why the boy's words bothered him. He tells me the boy was unjust. I ask Seth how he feels about justice and how to achieve justice. After a few questions, Seth realizes that beating up the boy furthers the injustice, so he changes his mind. It doesn't take a lecture or a horrified, "But you're a Christian!" or an angry, "Don't you dare, not with the money I've spent on those braces!"

An opportunity for communication is a huge gift, a marvelous chance to allow our child to become fully known, by our being open to knowing them fully.

Communication was often the last thing I wanted to do with a member of the family. Sometimes I was angry. At other times, I was afraid of being hurt by what they might say. I always told myself that "someone has to be the adult" in the situation, and I'd defer my feelings to a later time when I could work them out so that I could allow communication when it was offered.

The dinner hour was vital for many years, until the boys were older and we became more fragmented through activities and work schedules. Richard never used the dinner hour to "lay down the law" or judge what his kids were saying. Instead, as the children shared about their individual days, Richard often jumped in with memories from his childhood, which the boys loved. Even though I was always part of the conversation, I worked hard to learn to listen.

Cleaning up after dinner at our house was never a struggle because we all continued talking as we worked. I was careful to suggest cleanup just as one of the boys was launching into a story or getting ready to give a punch line, but never while I was talking. They wouldn't interrupt themselves to argue with me, and soon we all would be in the kitchen with the table cleared, everyone pitching in to put away food or to scrape dishes. To this day, my sons almost always clean up from family dinners or even dinner parties without being asked.

Recently Seth and I were home alone and made a nice dinner for ourselves. The meal ended while we were engrossed in conversation, and before I knew it, I'd cleaned the entire kitchen while he watched. I was unaware of what had happened until he laughed at me. He'd caught on to what I'd always done and turned the tables.

To start my children talking, one of the family counselors we visited, Dr. Barnes, gave me a piece of wisdom that has served me well in every relationship I have had. He said that whenever I found myself with my stepchildren alone, often in the car, I could frame that situation with my words into a positive affirmation.

Dr. Barnes told me to turn to the child and say with all sincerity, "I'm so glad I have this time alone with you." Sometimes the only reason I could be sincere was because I was dealing with just one instead of both of them. But whatever I felt at the time, I learned to put into words. "I enjoy being with you." "I've been missing you because we haven't spent much time together lately, so this is great." "I appreciate you for going to the market…gas station…mall with me because it gives us time to be together." No matter my mood, I almost always could say, "I'm interested in what's up with you, so it's great to have this time together."

The first time I said anything like this I felt awkward and ridiculous, the same feeling as watching a way-too-mushy scene in a movie. But before long, I was even telling my girlfriends if we went out to shop or to have a cup of coffee, "I'm so glad we get to have this time together." I remember once trying to teach a friend of mine how to communicate with her child. She looked at me dumbfounded. "You do that to *me!*" she said. I probably do it to everyone.

The Bible says, "The worlds were framed by the word of God."[3] We frame our worlds with our words as well. Positive statements provided a safe environment and an open ear for the boys to start talking. My words made them feel worthwhile and important, not like tagalongs in my busy life or a "chore" I had to do, like taking them to the doctor or to soccer practice. Even though most of the time when I said it we were just running errands or doing some kind of chore, making such a statement did what Dr. Barnes said it would do. It framed an otherwise ordinary situation into a special moment.

Seth was often withdrawn, the opposite of his outgoing brother, so sometimes after telling him I was happy to be with him, if he didn't start talking, I'd mention his silence. "It seems like you're quiet today. I guess you don't feel like talking. Do you mind if I talk?" If I would acknowledge his silence—which is just another form of communication—and let him know he was accepted even when he was quiet, he often would start talking. He just needed a connection—an empathetic ear.

To protect these opportunities, I never used our random trips as a soapbox to lecture the boys. Instead, I reserved them as times for being open with the boys and letting them know it was their turn to talk.

Years after starting this, my friend Cris mentioned that boys tend to talk side by side, whereas girls are not intimidated by talking face to face. I've observed since then that adults fall into similar communication patterns. My girlfriends and I like to sit across from one another in restaurants talking, whereas men seem to talk while they're sitting side by side hunting deer, fishing, attending sporting events, watching television or engaging in an activity. Cris has a friend whose son wouldn't open up until she took him golfing one day. He talked all the way home, then told his mom he'd had a wonderful time. It's not a hard and fast rule, but I think my communicating while we were in the car or busy in the kitchen made it easier for my sons to talk.

Another method is to spend time with each child one-on-one asking them if there is a way to help them. I'd learned from my dad to talk to my children on neutral turf. Their bedroom is their domain, and often the living room as well as the master bedroom is perceived as the parents'. So when I wanted to talk, I made sure we went somewhere else. As teenagers, my brother and sister and

Building Unity

I called my dad's talks a "Coke ride" because generally he took us for a Coca-Cola. I did the same with my sons.

NEGATIVE COMMUNICATION

With all the emotions stepfamily members harbor, getting through to any one of them can become an unexpected chore. One time Richard and I had a "Coke talk" with the boys and asked how we could help them fulfill their part in our family. Seth said he would like more "positive reinforcement," and Josh asked for more "family times." I'll never forget their comments because I felt we were bending over backward to do both. Often Seth acted disinterested in positive reinforcement and didn't respond. Josh tried to turn "family times" negative by acting out as if to push us into discipline instead of relaxed enjoyment.

Communication involves both a sender and receiver. Until the receiver can understand the sender's meaning, good communication doesn't take place. In a stepfamily, this takes time. My stepsons didn't believe me, or even their father. Nothing positive we did got through because they couldn't believe we would do it *for them*. We had a joke that our family's idea of "quality time" was an hour at a video arcade. In reality, if we spent an hour at a video arcade, they would assume it was because *we* wanted to, not because we wanted to treat them. They didn't trust us to take care of them or to look out for their interests, so they grasped at taking care of themselves. For the same reason, they showed little appreciation toward us. What was there to appreciate when they didn't believe we were trying to help them?

One autumn we bought two pumpkins to carve as a family. We taught the boys why we wouldn't do anything with spooks or monsters in preparation for our family event. But when Richard and I both left the house, they carved the pumpkins themselves, put candles in them, lit the candles, then lit hair spray on their jeans and did other pyrotechnics in the backyard. We returned, and they thought we'd be proud because they had carved crosses into the pumpkins, not ghosts. Trust was going to be hard to win.

Less than two months later we had family discussions about the Christmas tree. One cold December afternoon, both boys were indoors for discipline. Richard and I, not wanting to feel we had to punish ourselves as well, left for the store and gym, returning later to quite a surprise. As soon as our car had turned the corner as we left, they must have left the house and walked to the nearby creek, which is a government-owned ecological preservation area, and cut down trees for their bedrooms. Each had dragged a tree home, put it up in his room and decorated it with ornaments from the Christmas boxes in the garage.

I can only imagine what it looked like to the neighbors to see these kids, who were supposed to have learned conservation in school, walking down the street as happy as could be, dragging their illegal trees from the preserve behind them. Did they think their dad wouldn't notice they had Christmas trees in their rooms? Or that they'd gone outdoors? It's hysterical to me today, but on that day, it was not good. The worst of it was, we had a care group from church meeting in our home that night, and we had to take care of the issue as well as prepare for company before the meeting began.

On both occasions, the children sabotaged communication and acted on profound mistrust. Regardless of what we told the boys, they didn't trust us. They believed that anything they would get depended on their own ingenuity—of which they had plenty— and if they didn't take care of it while we were gone, they wouldn't be allowed to when we were home.

Often children hurt by divorce or death feel a need to grasp at whatever they can for fear of having things stripped away from them. Children in stepfamilies may steal, even if they don't need anything and they know better. The mother is stunned to find her favorite sweater missing. The stepfather is enraged when his best putter can't be found. As long as children have the feeling of having been cheated, they can try to make up for it by cheating and stealing.

The majority of first divorces occur within the first few years of marriage. If the children are quite young at the time of the divorce, they may miss out on an ordinary stage of development. Taking a child through a stage he or she should have passed earlier requires love, patience and commitment. But it can be done. A child's emotional baggage is never a reason to give up on the child. If we'll do our part, God will do His part.

The issues Josh and Seth dealt with were extreme compared with most, yet to some degree every stepfamily faces the same. Each spouse needs good support from the other to face these, which requires a good marriage. A good marriage also depends on communication.

Nurturing a Marriage

An embroidered decorator pillow in a gift shop reads, "Having kids is like being pecked to death by a chicken." All parents understand that. We all go through it. One time each, Richard and I lost control with each other. I screamed. He raged. But we didn't do it at the same time, which was good because the calm one helped bring back our equilibrium.

Troubled children can affect a stepfamily marriage far more than a nuclear family marriage. Parents join together to help a problem child in a nuclear family, but blended family parents are tempted to turn on each other. The stepparent is critical, the biological parent defensive. The stepparent blames, the biological parent protects, and they back each other into a pit of marriage quicksand.

Children are not affected as much when parents fight in a

stepfamily as they are in a nuclear family. They're not saying, "Mommy, Daddy, don't fight!" Instead they might be in their rooms laughing as they listen through the walls saying, "Hurrah, she's getting rid of him!"

Experts say stepfamily spouses must do three things. First, they must merge their family vision. Second, they must decide how to parent the children. If both spouses are to parent the child, the step-parent must creep into that precarious role over several years. The introduction period for stepmothers into a father's home seems faster, although I haven't found any research to confirm that. It would seem that since women are expected to fulfill nurturing responsibilities, the children find it easier to accept them. Third, spouses must nurture their own relationship.[4]

Marital satisfaction and the degree of personal happiness each spouse feels are two of three major markers used in Dr. Bray's study for determining the health of a stepfamily.[5] The third marker is the psychological and emotional development of the children. It is interesting that the first two are within the control of the spouses, even if their children don't cooperate. That means a healthy marriage between healthy adults contributes two-thirds of what it takes to create a healthy stepfamily. Of the two, I had 100 percent control of my half of them. I couldn't control others or situations, but I could control myself and my reactions to situations.

COMMUNICATION BEGINS BETWEEN HUSBAND AND WIFE

In any marriage—one involving a nuclear family or one involving a blended family—communication must first be developed and nurtured between a husband and wife.

The order given in the Bible is that before there is a child, there is a marriage. God didn't create a baby. He created an adult. The adults He created then had babies. The implication is, before dealing with the children, the adults need to be squared away. To do that, an ever-expanding library of great material on marriage exists.

Richard and I are certain we survived the tumultuous years of the initial "blend" because we concentrated on ourselves, not just the children. One thing Richard did as a biological parent that was crucial for me was to tell me not to worry about the kids. He would thank me for accepting his children into my life and would tell me I didn't have to do anything but be there. "None of us expect it," he said. It was as if all he expected was that I not kill them, which, although it was difficult at times, I also hoped to accomplish. By removing expectations, Richard gave me tremendous freedom. Superwoman died. The real woman emerged. I acted on my own, using what I had worked out with the Lord in prayer. Granted, Richard did have a vision for how our family would operate, but he was open to what part I would play within that vision. This was a giant gift to a stepparent.

We also did healthy things for ourselves. In the beginning of our marriage, Richard and I concentrated on learning how to communicate. After a series of arguments as newlyweds, we decided that we each would sit on one of the salmon-colored couches in our living room, which I'd had as a single woman. We each took a pen and pad, and with that physical distance helping, we tried to separate ourselves emotionally. Then we set the rules. We would only use "I" statements. Instead of "You always" or "You said that" we said, "My perception is," or "In my opinion."

Richard started first, talking about anything he wanted until he couldn't think of anything else. I made a few notes instead of interrupting. At first he talked for maybe fifteen minutes. When it was my turn, I took thirty. Then he went again, and it stretched on and on and on, but we refused to leave until we were all talked out. The first one lasted more than four hours, and by the end of it we felt as if we'd just taken a long shower. It was exhilarating.

CAN STEPFAMILIES BE DONE RIGHT?

The boys came to live with us, and we still scheduled time for "couch talks," either when they were away or sitting on the bed and the chair in the bedroom. Back and forth we would go as we clarified, tabled or settled issues. We talked out our differences, aired our grievances, found common ground and remembered why we fell in love in the first place.

Relaxing and having fun as a couple, not a family, was also crucial, even if it was just an inexpensive date for an evening. A year after the boys came, my parents helped us take a real vacation. We winged our way to Cancun, Mexico, for five glorious days—which felt like five months. We didn't even talk about the boys the whole time we were gone, and we felt great. The day we left for Mexico, Seth ran away from a day school we'd found for the boys that summer. The school called the police, and Seth still regales us with the story of how he almost outran them on foot, even though they were in cars. He'd felt rejected and afraid, and had acted out his feelings. But his negative reaction couldn't deter us from continuing to take time for ourselves.

We refused to become hostages to our own children. It's not healthy for parents, nor for children, to allow children to wield that kind of power. We just reassured Seth the next time that we weren't rejecting him and that we could be trusted to return.

Money cannot buy everything, but sometimes it can buy sanity! If stepparents have the resources, time away from the children is critical. The biological parent usually won't sense this need as great as the stepparent. Trust the stepparent.

Besides working on our marriage, Richard and I took care of our mental health. As soon as we gained custody of the boys, I registered for a genealogy course at a Dallas university. It took more than an hour to get there, which was to me like slipping *out* of the Twilight Zone. I'd see the freeway exits fly by for the soccer fields, the orthodontist, the school, and I'd keep driving, alone in the car, rushing to some place where no one knew my stepsons and where they couldn't follow. Freedom!

Richard eventually enrolled in school full time and often studied through the dinner hour, leaving me alone with the boys. For years Richard also dealt with depression, and although it doesn't happen anymore, at the time it would sometimes blanket him, forcing him to withdraw almost completely from the family for a while. It wasn't easy, but I refused to begrudge him his depression or his schooling. His being able to have a mental health break or enjoy life apart from the family was important to him, and it contributed to keeping our marriage healthy.

Broaden Communication to Include the Kids

As for the psychological and emotional health of our children, we failed on that marker. Through their emotional cyclones flashed bolts of brilliance, and they seemed at times to be wonderful kids. But the cyclone would not stop. *Pathological* means "altered by disease." I kept thinking that if I could just find the disease, I could also find a cure. I tried everything. I called nutritionists, doctors, schools, research universities and government and privately sponsored resources for "borderline" kids. We invited all our friends who had ever dealt with demon possession to come over and spend time with the kids. If only it had "just" been a demon, they could have cast it out, and we could have gone on our merry way! We terrified parents as we tried various private schools, exposing their well-adjusted children to our little wonders.

We went for family counseling many times. One counselor told us we could hospitalize one of the boys in a psychiatric ward. I didn't feel it was right to subject him to that, since I figured he'd think of it as his parents locking him up. Worse, he might decide he was a "psycho." He didn't need any more ideas. I also didn't want to subject him to the spiritual warfare that would no doubt be tremendous in such a place. Richard and I rejected the idea. If we didn't have money for family counseling, we went to our pastor. We exhausted every resource. We found a day school one summer that was covered by our insurance. It helped Josh catch up on some school subjects while counselors used behavior-modification methods to try to straighten them both out. The boys were able to pass some classes that their schools accepted as credit, although they didn't seem to get much out of the counseling. It was a counselor at that school who "helped" the boys with their aggression by suggesting that I would be the object of that aggression. Those particular counselors were better at dealing with adolescents alone than within the children's families.

In addition to damaged emotions, we dealt with adjustments every stepfamily makes. Day-to-day jolts and shocks from the effort to "blend" can wound each family member even when every member is trying to nurture the relationship. Seth and I describe these as "emotional bumps."

EMOTIONAL BUMPING

Honeymooners spend the first months and perhaps years of marriage discovering each other's tastes and differences. The thrill of taking him to his first Japanese restaurant. The laughter at seeing her play her first game of foosball. Every time we discover something new, we say things like, "Oh, you don't like baloney sandwiches. Well, neither do I!" Or, "Uh-oh, you're not a make-the-bed-in-the-morning person. I guess I'll do that."

We merge our lives with a pretty good attitude, even if it's annoying, because we're "in love." We discover each other's history, desires, habits, likes and dislikes. Sometimes we don't like what we find, but we don't feel betrayed by it. It was just something we found in the other person that we didn't like. We deal with it. When children come, they are a wonder to the couple, and both parents have the opportunity to learn the child's personality together. "He doesn't like beets." "She has a strong will." "He loves animals." "She likes to play airplane."

In a stepfamily, however, such differences in tastes, personalities and routines tend to rub against other family members and serve to remind the members that, no matter how hard everyone is trying or how much you love each other, you're still only a "starter" family. Children have already been developed by another parent, whose ideas about parenting may be very different from the stepparent's ideas of parenting. The child has to answer to those inner "ghosts," and to the new parent as well.

Emotional bumps are innocent ways we communicate something that goes against the grain of another family member. They are frustrating in a stepfamily because the members don't have a honeymooner's emotional charge of feeling "in love," which could help them through. Most emotional bumps come across as some kind of betrayal, as if a husband discovered his wife didn't like camping and had put up with it just to please him. Or she found out he didn't like her meatloaf but said he did for her. Such discoveries are uncomfortable at best, wounding at worst.

For example, an emotional bump could come if part of the family grew up eating their mashed potatoes with skins on and now a family member is sitting at Thanksgiving dinner unable or unwilling to eat potatoes that haven't been peeled. Both the cook and the noneater feel the rub, and it's an emotional issue instead of just a matter of individual taste. Both have that odd sense of being betrayed by the other.

Instead of discovering differences in a good-natured way, each "bump" seems to scream, "THIS IS NOT A REAL FAMILY!" As much as we want the adjustment period to end, as hard as we try, as much as we want to be "real," the bump comes, and we're once again hurt or frustrated. Emotions are feelings, not rational thoughts, so trying to talk people out of the feeling by using reason is frustrating to them. The feeling that "nobody understands" sets in. Solving the choice of whether we'll have peeled potatoes or potatoes with skins is no longer the issue when emotions engage.

These innocent differences bothered my family. Things that in any other setting would not carry an emotional charge now did. One time, as I was preparing dinner, I asked Seth if he wanted the peaches or the fruit cocktail. He gave an honest and inoffensive answer. "You know I don't like canned peaches."

As irrational as it was, I felt hurt because I didn't know or didn't remember that he didn't like canned peaches. I had to control my emotions and say to myself, "It's just a stupid can of peaches."

As for sack lunches, I could not force myself to make the boys' lunches if they were sitting able-bodied in the next room watching television or fiddling with the stereo or goofing around. That made no sense to me. So, unless they were busy with homework or after-school sports or something, I told them to make their own. This was small, but it was still something they'd never had to do before, and it reminded them every day that they weren't living with their mom anymore.

The way we cleaned house, our ritual for going to bed at night, the fact that Richard didn't play Nintendo with them, how we celebrated birthdays—just about anything—could "bump" and jostle us, unnerving us and leaving irritations and abrasions. One time Josh and I got into an enormous argument over a can of pea soup. *Pea soup!*

Another time I did what I'd grown up doing in my "family of origin"—I favored a guest over my own kids. We were playing a game, but there were too many people, so I asked Josh to create a "team" with someone else, while making another teenager Josh's age a team on his own. This embarrassed Josh because he thought

I was making a value judgment, like he wasn't good enough to play the game on his own.

As we worked it out alone later, even Richard didn't take my side. I'd never even considered that not every family favored guests over family members. My family just always had. For Richard and Josh this was a new thing, and for Josh it had been very hurtful because he felt it as a keen rejection. I've since come around to their way of thinking, at least somewhat, and have not expected my kids to make the same sacrifices that being in a minister's family had always required of me.

These bumps *will* go away, and the family *will* function. With time, little things that come up no longer have the emotional impact they once had. And as familiarity grows, individuals will begin to feel like a family. I remember going to a hospital with Seth recently and looking through the nursery windows at the babies. Lost in watching the infants, Seth said, "What time was I born?" Lost in thought myself, I started thinking back, then realized I wasn't the possessor of such information.

A moment later he looked at me, still waiting for an answer but I just smiled. As we looked at each other, he realized what he'd asked, and we both laughed. It was an innocent mistake, a funny one, and neither of us felt bad about it. But had that happened in the beginning, either one of us might have felt a tinge of emotion.

FLUSHING THE SYSTEM

Good communication depends on a good attitude underneath. We communicate by word, gesture and spirit. The spirit underneath our communication speaks louder than any words. One of the greatest keys to clear attitudes is forgiveness. Applying forgiveness is like flushing the cesspool of life. Forgiveness allows us to take every rotten, stinking thing that anyone has brought into our lives, including what we ourselves have done, and get rid of it for good.

CAN STEPFAMILIES BE DONE RIGHT?

Jesus Christ came to this earth with a mission to forgive. He didn't wait for people to file past His cross and say, "Sorry." He forgave. Freely. Generously. Richly. Magnanimously. He completed His work on this earth by uttering the greatest three words ever spoken, "Father, forgive them." These were an outgrowth of His love and, in that moment, superseded even, "I love you." Had He not forgiven, after all He'd gone through on our behalf, we still would not be able to enter heaven. It is only by receiving Christ's forgiveness that heaven is open to us. As my dad says, forgiveness opens. Unforgiveness closes.

People misunderstand forgiveness. Forgiveness from the heart doesn't need a request. We forgive because God's Word tells us to and because we've been forgiven ourselves, not just because somebody asked for it. Forgiveness from the heart may take more than one solitary act of forgiving. Sometimes uttering the words the first time is only a first step. We forgive "seventy times seven," as Jesus told the apostles, in order to clean the offense from our hearts for good.

Richard and I spent about a year forgiving people just to clear our pasts from our lives. We forgave Scout leaders, piano teachers, coaches, acquaintances, doctors, friends, former boyfriends and girlfriends. It wasn't that we'd been "right" all our lives and everyone else was "wrong." It was that the little offenses we held from childhood had never been resolved. We couldn't trust that we were pure and clear in our hearts and minds because of hundreds of past perceptions that sat stagnating within us. We flushed them out through forgiveness.

One day in prayer, Richard forgave the boys' mother and stepfather, and everyone that had anything to do with his divorce, including himself. He became overwhelmed with compassion and cried out in prayer on behalf of his former wife. I was in another part of the house, but his voice carried as he began to cry.

Building Unity

It moved me to hear him. I realized I was angry too, because I felt like an innocent bystander who was called in to pay for a crime. That was important to realize. The principle is, "You can't heal a wound by saying it isn't there." If we don't acknowledge what is in our own hearts, we can't apply forgiveness and become free. My anger would have shown up in unhealthy ways toward my children, Richard, the Other Parents and myself. I forgave the Other Parents many times until I felt it from my heart. When they started showing up in my dreams sitting down for a meal with us, laughing and talking together, I knew I had forgiven. The dream might never become a reality, but at least my heart was open to that reality.

I forgave Richard and the boys each day, not always because of something in particular, but because I knew I had exposed my subconscious mind to the opportunity to feel offended, slighted and rejected. I refused to allow those feelings to accumulate, so I got rid of them during my regular time of prayer.

With Josh and Seth both, we worked on forgiveness. The biggest problem for them was to acknowledge that anything had happened. Seth repressed his emotions and would cover for other family members saying, "It wasn't so bad." Denial, which is just lying to yourself, was easier than facing the pain. Richard and I were somewhat handicapped because we didn't want to create a scapegoat on which to hang the boys' problems, but they needed to understand the violation that took place so they could forgive.

People get upset for just about any reason. The traffic. The slow or inaccurate bank teller. The company that recalled our tires. The weather. As Mark Twain said, "Everyone complains about the weather, but no one does anything about it."

My feeling is that life isn't long enough and the world too big for us to fuss and fume about every little thing. It wouldn't take two seconds to think of how privileged and fortunate we are.

CAN STEPFAMILIES BE DONE RIGHT?

Some people just need to drive through a homeless area or turn on the evening news or take a trip overseas. *If living in a blended family is our biggest problem, we should bend over and kiss the ground every day of our lives and thank God that's the biggest issue we face.* Some people send their children out to find food or water each day and don't know if they'll ever see them again. Others watch people starve around them and can do nothing to help. We *can* find it in our hearts to forgive those around us and to appreciate all God has given us.

Every member of the family needs to forgive. A friend of mine who had just married moved his new wife and her children into his home with his children. Both my friend and his wife are educated, dedicated and responsible people, but no matter what his wife did with his children, they resented her and disobeyed her. His children's biological mother had died, and they channeled a great deal of emotion into negative behavior toward "The Imposter."

Father and stepmother continued to love and administer discipline without favoring her children over his, and they stuck to a sound parenting plan. They also took frequent getaways to refresh their love and commitment to each other. After a few years, his oldest son had a dramatic turnaround and realized he was at war with his stepmother because he blamed her for his mother's death. Even though his anger was unfounded, he needed to forgive his stepmother for something she didn't even do! The boy realized he was mad at God as well, and even "forgave" God. God didn't need to be forgiven, but forgiveness is for the forgiver, and through forgiveness the boy released pent-up anger and emotions. The boy's sister never did forgive, and the divergent paths their lives have taken as young adults make it plain which is living free and which is still in the bondage of unforgiveness.

The Bible says Jesus "breathed" on the disciples after He rose from the dead and said, "If you forgive the sins of any, they are forgiven them; if you retain the sins of any, they are retained."[6] Sometimes all the bile is backed up in our hearts because we've retained others' actual sins by our lack of forgiveness. Often it's not just their sins, but the spirit in which they sinned against us that pollutes our own spirits.

In our forgiving, we have to forgive ourselves. We will not live to a ripe old age with peace and happiness and a house filled with joy if we don't clean the garbage out of our hearts. It may take weeks or months to come to grips with something we've done wrong, or something that's been done against us. But we'll never be able to live with ourselves if we don't forgive the biggest problem—ourselves.

The mistakes I made in my stepfamily hurt not just me but all of us, and I would have loved going back to do certain things over or take back words I'd spoken. Doctors bury their mistakes. Ministers and teachers send theirs home. We parents have to live with ours. The only way I could was by forgiving myself. And continuing to forgive myself every time a stray thought brought the deed back again. I'll tell you later about the greatest mistake I ever made with my kids. It was innocent enough, but it brought tremendous grief. Forgiveness was the core of my survival.

SETH— My stepmom and dad always laughed at the funny things I did and encouraged my talent in art. My stepmom always encouraged whatever I did, as long as it was somewhat productive. Even when I was skateboarding, the "degenerate kid" sport, my stepmom came out on the porch to watch me do new tricks. I always thought that was cool because even my brother wasn't that interested in my abilities. There were always these late-night conversations with my stepmom when I'd tell her something or show her something, and she'd say, "Good, Seth!" Except the way she says it is "Goo—ood..." If it wasn't a school or work night, we'd talk for hours, sometimes until early the next morning.

Even in communicating, I had a negative filter. My perceptions of what my parents were saying were always different from what they meant. Even though my parents encouraged productivity in my life, I didn't produce. Negativity had such a strong grip on my life that it took unbelievable amounts of positive reinforcement to counterbalance that. The results were years in coming, but they did come.

My parents were always consistent in their positive reinforcement of the good things I did, no matter how many bad things I had going on. After I was arrested for drugs and kicked out of my house, I came back to ask if I could stay with them until the court date. My dad and I sat down and discussed it. He had me write out my own plan. I showed him that I was serious, and he saw it. He encouraged me by allowing me to move back home, but under stricter-than-normal rules. Even after the grief I'd put them through and complete disregard for the rules, they saw me doing something positive in my life and encouraged it.

I never had a problem in deciding what my parents didn't like, compared with what they did like. They were always clear in what they expected from me. This had a major impact on me. I didn't know where I stood with my friends most of the time, but I always knew with my parents. It never surprised me when they got upset at something that I did wrong. In fact, I usually knew ahead of time that what I was planning to do would upset them. As a child, this led me to become skilled in the art of lying.

Lying is negative communication. Relationships cannot progress when you're lying. If I had taken time to be honest with my feelings, then my parents would not have had to spend so much time trying to find out what I was thinking. Everything they did was an attempt to help me. To help me, my parents needed to know me. I made that difficult.

I was upset every time they introduced discipline or took me to counseling because I didn't want to open up. Dealing with those feelings was just too difficult. I couldn't find a comfort zone, a sense of peace. My actions said what I was feeling: "Leave me alone and let me do what I want."

Not dealing with my emotions turned out to be a lot harder than just being honest and letting them help. It still would have been hard, but not as hard as spending so much time and energy in hiding.

Keeping my emotions to myself ate me alive. Bottled feelings warped my thoughts and actions. I didn't see things clearly. I had no hope. I was full of disgust with happy, bubbly people and wished that their lives would be riddled with problems like mine. I should have been curious about why they were that way and figured out how to stop having problems in my life. That never occurred to me.

Two times I remember being overwhelmed by emotions. Once was when I was young. I don't remember what had upset me, but I shut myself in my room, took off all my clothes, laid between the sheets of my bed and seethed in anger. I spent every ounce of my energy to keep from losing control of my emotions. I was so overwhelmed that I could do nothing but focus on repressing my anger. That was such an awful thing to put myself through. I was so knotted up emotionally and physically that I couldn't even fall asleep. I just lay there awake for hours. The next morning I still had that anger in me, it was just repressed. It didn't give me a solution, just a method of coping.

The second time was during a drug experience. My brother, a few friends and I took some ecstasy, then went to the lake to hang out while we were high. While there, my friend Phil and I discussed life as children of divorce. Ecstasy is an emotion-enhancing drug. It causes you to feel emotions stronger than you normally would. Phil was going through his parents' divorce after a twenty-three-year marriage. As we got more and more in-depth about our emotions, I

85

opened up to him like I had never opened up to anyone before. We both laughed and cried, and despite the drug's influence, I felt relieved to have a lot of those emotions off my chest.

In both of those situations I dealt with the overwhelming emotions I had bottled up inside myself. The first way was to repress it, and the second was to release it. The second way was the only way that brought relief, and yet the only reason I let those emotions out with Phil was because of the drug. I wouldn't recommend that to anyone. Phil died while living that lifestyle. I had just started sobering up, but I was too late to help Phil. While he was alive, Phil and I developed a relationship in which we could talk on an intimate level and share our feelings without the influence of drugs. Those moments were the most beneficial to me, and those memories are some of my best.

My parents were always open to talk. They were nonjudgmental when I did open up to them. They let me speak freely and openly whenever I wanted to, and they would drop whatever they were doing to give that attention when I was ready to talk. I rarely took advantage of those opportunities, but when I did, we all took giant steps forward in becoming a closer family and resolving our problems. That had a huge impact on me.

4

PEOPLE NEED PEOPLE

JOANN— It seems that if just two parents were involved with two or five or seventeen children between them, the family could learn to live together in harmony. But instead, most blended families have more family members than they know what to do with.

The children might have four sets of grandparents, plus the grandparents of any stepbrothers and stepsisters. The grandparents may have been divorced, so there could be eight sets instead of four. Along with the expanding number of grandparents come more aunts, uncles and cousins. Then there are extended families with second cousins, third cousins once-removed and so on. In genealogy, second marriages can make family trees into something more like bushes or entire hedgerows.

My sister Lois, the lawyer, once lived in a small town where people were pretty much all related to one another. If not by blood, they were related by a previous marriage or a brother's or

87

sister's marriage. It made jury selection a real trick. Lois had to ask a court secretary, who had grown up there, to point out on the jury list all the relationships between jurors, lawyers, police officers and the accused. Blended families have a tendency to spread out that way, and depending on who becomes close to whom, they can become either awkward or a huge blessing.

I remember one Christmas when Josh and Seth's Other Parents lived near Richard's family. We spent our holiday driving the boys from house to house. Richard's parents were divorced, so we had two celebrations to attend on his side, then we joined my family at my sister's. At one point, I turned around to the boys riding in the back seat and said, "I'm sorry we have to do all this driving." Without a moment's pause they said, "No problem! We get more presents this way!"

"Extra" people in stepfamilies provide more opportunities not only for children to receive presents but also for parents to have more babysitters and more adults showing an interest in the children's lives. Every parent knows how hard it is to find a Scout leader, music teacher, schoolteacher or coach who will take a special interest in a child. Having more people available to form a vested interest in our children can be a tremendous benefit to a stepfamily. "There is a lot of room in a child's life for love, affection and respect," writes one stepfamily expert. "There is no limit to the number of adults who can provide these precious qualities.[1]

A friend of mine involved in a gifted-children's school said the results of the school's informal survey showed that every child who excels has at least four adults concerned with the child's life. I like a "magic number" to work toward, but even without it, the simple truth is that parents are people who need people.

The only downside to the extended stepfamily is that each family member comes with his or her own set of expectations and prejudices. Some believe the parents should never have divorced, so they won't spend time with the new family. Others don't like the way the new children in the family act or how they haven't already "blended" into the language, customs and habits of the family. Through often unspoken communication, they make a child feel unwanted, as if the child wasn't raised in that family.

Stepfamilies cannot force other family members to accept their new family. Most of my family struggled with my children's misbehavior. They didn't know the half of it because I didn't tell them everything for fear of alienating my kids even further from them. But I shared enough, and they saw enough for it to be upsetting.

My dad, who is a minister, did not approve of much of what my boys did. But he exercised forgiveness, which kept his heart open. Josh and Seth felt guilty and awkward around him, but he didn't rub it in. The boys came to a decision to conform to better morals and values, and my dad was there to start their relationship anew. Seth even ended up working for him and appeared in public with him a few times, which was a tremendous help for Seth's spiritual maturity—and I think for his self-esteem as well.

My mother bonded more with Josh, particularly later, when my parents moved to Texas. Josh would go over to help her with odd jobs around the house. Josh ended up leaving Texas for more than four years, and when he returned Mom picked right back up with him again. She had a special place in her heart for him, and he needed that. She was herself the embodiment of the words "mercy" and "grace." Even though she often tired of my boys' antics, she never judged or condemned them. The boys were going through something pretty serious one time, and I'll never forget her comment. "We can't blame them for their youthfulness," she said. What an inspiration!

Adjusting Expectations

Every member of the extended family needs to work out his or her relationship with the stepmembers. The parents' role is to understand other family members' points of view and win them over to the parents' point of view. As adults, we have the power to communicate with one another and help others adjust their expectations. We can bring people into line with our children's actual capabilities and create a single united vision for the lives of our children.

I'll never forget Mr. Cook, Seth's science teacher, calling me one day after another raucous incident in the classroom and saying, "Can't you make Seth mind?" He saw what looked like a "good" family on the outside and couldn't understand the behavior he saw on the inside.

We'd had custody of the children for less than a year, and I didn't even want to answer. I just wanted to cry. The first thing that came to my mind was Seth's anthem, "It's not my fault." I struggled throughout much of the conversation because I wanted to accept responsibility and face the problem head-on, not duck behind "reasons" that might be mere excuses.

It's a chore not to blame everything that happens in a child's life on The Divorce or the Other Parents. Blaming others allows us to escape our own responsibility in the situation. It also strips personal power from the child and takes away the child's sense of responsibility for his or her own actions. Allowing a child to say "I'm the way I am because . . ." implies that the child has no power to change. Although this feels good to a child at first, taken to the extreme it is fatalism and teaches him or her to act like a victim.

I told Mr. Cook that we'd only had custody a few months and that we were experiencing behavior problems at home as well. Then I said that in no way did I believe this meant Seth should be catered to or given a lower standard than other children, but that it just was going to take time. As a result, he switched Seth's class times to separate him from his friend Randy.

Mr. Cook understood the difference between vision and expectation. Mr. Cook and I both envisioned Seth's passing his science class. But as an experienced teacher, he realized it was unrealistic to expect Seth to pass under the current circumstances. After Mr. Cook knew the background, he realized that sticking it out wasn't going to bring a resolution within one semester. I thought he had a good and fair solution. I didn't want to change the rules to serve the inability of the kids, but I also didn't want to set them up for certain failure.

Parents have to understand that our vision of children who are well-adjusted, positive citizens who live with us in a harmonious stepfamily is a good vision and is something worthwhile to hope for and toward which we can work. That's our vision, yet it likely will not happen right now or today. That's our expectation.

The higher the aspiration of the parent, the higher the child's own aspirations. I wanted to aspire to greatness and for my children to do the same, but I had to reconcile that vision with the reality of where we were, which was anything but great. *As stepfamily parents, we have to be able to lower our expectations without giving up our dreams.*

I refused to change the vision I had for my kids just because they acted for a while like hoodlums. Both showed flashes of brilliance in various areas. Seth was artistic, witty and eloquent. Even his stubbornness seemed like it would one day serve him well when he applied it to persevering instead of quitting. Josh was the organizer and natural-born leader, a real talker but also a "doer." He misused his skills at times, like when he organized what seemed like half the school to attend a rock festival, then tried to play sick that Sunday morning so he could join them. The problem was, it was Easter Sunday, and we found out what he was doing.

It's up to the parents to see the seed of greatness in our kids through whatever disguise our children have given it. They go out for tennis, and we believe on their behalf that they could one day win Wimbledon if they chose. But our expectation, based on their mental and emotional state, is that it will be great if they show up for practice.

Parents can dream big, but must reward every small step the child takes in the right direction. I've seen parents and professionals make the big mistake of "dumbing down" standards. It's better to maintain high standards and adjust expectations to fit the child by rewarding incremental improvements. Richard and I had read about dumbing down, but we learned it firsthand from Ricky, a troubled teen who became one of our "adopted" sons.

Ricky learned from the institutions where he'd spent much of his young life that if he was horrid, then over time the professionals in charge would reduce the requirements to help him pass. He learned it was worthwhile to be as bad as he could be. This is similar to parents who tell a child they'll give him or her a Popsicle if the child will stop screaming. They inadvertently reward a screaming child, which ensures the child will keep screaming. Big mistake.

INSPIRING RESPONSIBILITY

Our children need to learn to accept responsibility for their actions. They need adults to believe in them, not make excuses on their behalf. "Give others a good reputation to live up to," is one of Dale Carnegie's principles in his classic *How to Win Friends & Influence People*. I assigned that book as summer reading for the boys one year, and had them create a rap tune out of the principles. They read halfheartedly, performed their song wholeheartedly, and each came away with just a little more understanding about life.

Refreshing myself on the principles, I realized that I could either beat down my kids when they acted out with, "You're a big, bad...," or I could uplift them with, "You're better than the way you're acting." The second statement conveys that the child needs to become accountable for the greatness that lies within him or her.

Some people are geniuses when it comes to child rearing. One of my heroes is Monty Roberts, the original "Horse Whisperer." He has taken his principles for horse taming and exercised them on child rearing, proving his theories by taking into his home and rehabilitating damaged and abused children, often teens.

Monty teaches people to treat horses with patience and respect, not "breaking" them. His method of gentling a horse is used worldwide, whereby a would-be rider befriends the horse by "speaking" in the horse's language through body language. The horse and rider enter an "agreement" whereby the horse does as commanded because the rider has made it pleasant to do so.

With children, Monty believes in respecting them, setting parameters and defining expectations. After that "agreement" is set, he believes in allowing the child to fail. If the child fulfills the agreement, rewards come along the way, but if he disobeys, natural consequences that he has agreed to then take over. The parent doesn't say the child must obey because otherwise the parent will hurt him or her. Instead, if the child doesn't meet realistic expectations, he will hurt himself. Of forty-seven young people who were "adopted" by Monty on his horse ranch, forty became productive citizens.

CREATING A NETWORK

Another person I admire is H. Stephen Glenn, who has spent a lifetime studying, analyzing, and teaching educators and parents how to raise productive children. A tremendous opportunity came when he served President Jimmy Carter in the White House. He was given access to every study ever done on children—from studies on their health to their gang involvement, housing, education, nutrition and thousands more. He was able to dissect and cross-examine the various materials and meld them into a philosophy that he has taught all over the country.

I read his books and heard him speak at our local high school and discovered that his mother was a wonderful Christian woman whose prayers I'm sure contributed to his success. His book, *Raising Self-Reliant Children in a Self-Indulgent World,* is terrific.[2] Like Monty, he raised his own children, plus at least twenty other troubled teens.

In his book, Dr. Glenn outlines how children from a previous era were healthier when extended families lived together and worked a ranch or farm. He figured that we would not be moving back to the farm anytime soon, but we could still make changes to our urban lifestyles that would recreate that same environment. Dr. Glenn names four critical factors that we can bring back today even though we did not live on the farm with an extended family.

- A network
- Meaningful roles
- On-the-job training for life
- Parenting resources[3]

We'll get back to his first point, and the last just means the tools available to parents, but here's a quick synopsis of the others. "Meaningful roles" comes from the fact that most children today do not believe that they contribute to the well-being of the family or community. Dr. Glenn suggests making them "significant con-tributors," not "passive recipients." I have noticed in my children and those they attracted to our home that they often feel extra-neous to what is going on, like they don't count. They think what they do shouldn't have any effect on anyone else in the home. It's as if they feel invisible.

The "on-the-job training for life" is the idea that children are learning more through media today than through hands-on experience. I felt that introducing my children to a variety of experiences was the best way for them to discover their strengths, preferences, talents and to choose a career. I also believed the psalmist who wrote, "I will make the godly of the land my heroes, and invite them to my home," so I often had people over to dinner, not just for their friendship, but to expose my children to them.[4] From these experiences, Seth chose to pursue Web design, combining his brains and artistic ability. Josh chose to pursue culinary arts, which utilizes his creativity, courage to experiment and ability to organize.

A *network* meant a group of people who worked together to bring up the child, which Dr. Glenn says is essential to social functioning. "In the absence of a network culture, it is essential to actively learn to create substitutes for those that originally occurred spontaneously."[5]

After reading Dr. Glenn's book, I made a point of meeting all our neighbors. I'm basically an introvert, so going door to door was a huge challenge. As my kids grew and neighbors moved, I never did it again, and I feel a pang of guilt to admit that. But for a season it was worthwhile for the children, and I'm glad I did it.

My children would be busy with school projects, or perhaps cooking something, and I encouraged them to go to neighbors' houses to "borrow a cup of sugar" or to ask their participation in their project, just to create that sense of community. And since we had two big boys living in our house, neighbors called on them to help move furniture and dig ditches. This was very healthy, as it created some nearby help and accountability that acted as a security blanket in all our minds.

I remember one time when the neighbors rallied to help Seth. He was smart enough to pass tests without studying, but when it came to things like taking a paper to school, he was lazy. One day Richard was driving the morning carpool to the private school where Seth was enrolled, when all the kids loaded into the van with giant pieces of cardboard mounted with science papers for the science fair.

Richard questioned Seth about his project, which we'd never heard about, and discovered that Seth hadn't done one. Richard told Seth to come home with a piece of cardboard. Even though the best Seth could hope for was to receive a full grade lower for being late, we told him he had to do the project.

That afternoon Seth painted his board and, because he had the artistic touch, it looked terrific. Inspired, he went around to neighbors' houses to experiment on how different types of music affected their powers of concentration.

He received a *B* for the work, which only took him one evening to put together from start to finish. This sparked awe in classmates who worked for a month to get their *B,* and created a new understanding in Seth's mind that if he would put out a little effort, he could do well, and might even enjoy doing it.

Academics aside, by calling on nearby neighbors to help in a time of need, Seth received the impression that people were on all sides who cared and would support him. That was as important a lesson as any schoolwork.

Besides the neighbors, we also became involved in a church where people took an interest in our children. I'll never forget my shock when I arrived at one of Josh's softball games late, only to discover his Sunday school teacher and youth leader had come to his game. The support of caring adults couldn't erase every difficulty, but together we were fighting an uphill battle with time as our ally.

Sometimes parents just need to know other people are helping share the load. It's like the Internet joke about the guy whose truck got stuck in a ditch outside a farm. The farmer said his mule "Blue" could pull the truck free. The farmer hitched Blue to the truck and said, "Pull, Blue." No movement. "Pull, Elmer." The truck budged. "Pull, Biscuit." The truck was free. The man asked the farmer why he called his mule by three different names. "Simple," said the farmer. "Blue is blind. And if he thought he was the only one pulling, your truck would still be in the ditch!"

Our own network of friends was a big part of our family's adjustment. As parents, we need people who will support us as we get through those crazy first couple of years. We had friends who stayed with or checked up on the kids if we were away, and who took the boys out on their own "Coke rides" to help them through certain problems.

We didn't have the greatest network established at first, but it developed as casual friends lent an ear and became closer by walking through our difficulties with us. Sometimes, though, I could tell my friends and family were worn out with hearing about the boys' latest antics. That's when my friends who were out of town became a huge support.

FRIENDS

One area where parents have little control, and are able to exercise influence only from a distance, is with their children's friends, particularly school friends with whom the parents have little contact. One of Seth's friends had a terrible relationship with his stepfather. Whenever Seth was with this boy, Seth's attitude would alter. He would be rude to me, make sarcastic remarks and sort of throw his head back with a curled-lip, devil-may-care, Elvis sort of look. It looked ridiculous on a fourteen-year-old. Eventually I'd see that look and say, "Seen Chris lately?" Of course he'd just spent the afternoon with the boy, and he'd wonder how I knew.

Chris often became the source of conversation, as I made it my business to learn about this friend. From the sound of it, I would not have welcomed him into my home, nor would I have allowed Seth to spend time at his house, but that issue never arose. I just kept working on counterbalancing the negative impressions Chris was helping to create in Seth's mind. Because of some mistakes I made at the same time, I lost this battle.

Our house rules were that the boys could spend Friday nights at friends' homes, but not Saturday nights. Anyone who spent the night at our house on Saturday night had to come to church with us on Sunday morning. But this was a rule that was slow to form and slow to be applied. One of the pitfalls in stepfamilies is the change of rules between one household and the other. Stricter parents often are perceived as unyielding monsters. Richard and I learned to take our time.

We screened the friends with whom Seth became close. Of those he spent the night with, we met the parents or at least knew of them.

On one occasion an overnight guest seemed detrimental enough that Richard and I targeted the friendship in prayer. I talked with the child's mother by telephone and found her charming. Seth talked about the boy for well over a month, acting a little jealous because the boy was already filling out, whereas Seth, who was still gaining height, didn't have much meat on his bones. But when the child spent a Saturday night, Richard and I felt as if there was a strange chill in the air. We prayed, and the child suddenly left school for some kind of boarding school or rehabilitation center.

Years later Seth met up with a short young man by the same name who had messed himself up in drunk-driving wrecks and with drugs. After I questioned Seth as to whether this was the same boy, Seth asked him and was shocked to discover that he was.

We prayed by name for each of the children Josh and Seth mentioned or brought home. We saw some give their hearts to Christ.

Sometimes they didn't act on that conversion right away, but God did. Of those we still know, many are serving Christ today. Ryan runs the audio department of our church and works for my dad. Randy married a Christian friend's daughter, and they attend our old church. Ricky is in and out of our home still and attends our church. From time to time, Seth hears about old friends who have converted. He ran with a rough crowd, but I like to believe many made it because of prayers from that season of their lives.

To help counteract the negative effects of negative friends, Richard and I tried to have a greater influence on the children. I kept the boys busy with as many family activities as I could. We would sometimes include their friends, but not always. We went to Christian musicians' appearances at the local mall or to hear Christian sports heroes speak. We took them to concerts, foreign or classic films and professional ball games of all kinds when we could afford it, and went bowling, miniature golfing or to video arcades. We almost always had some kind of a project going, from watching all of Alfred Hitchcock's movies to decorating the boys' bedrooms. One Thanksgiving they went with our friend Doug Stringer to work at an orphanage in Mexico. They held bake sales, raked lawns and collected aluminum cans to earn money to go. It was a great experience start to finish.

I also didn't want our boys ever to feel they had to get married because they didn't know their way around a house, so I gave them opportunities to shop for and cook the family dinner. I taught them how to sew to make their own curtains for their bedrooms. Even though I did everyone's laundry, they asked to learn, eager to act like adults, and they learned to iron as well. They were proud of their skills, proud that they were more accomplished at household responsibilities than most kids their age.

Richard did the "manly" things—teaching weightlifting and about things like tools and cars. He also took private time with

them about personal hygiene and sex. We all went on family outings on summer weekends and vacations at least once a year,
often traveling cross-country by car. And we talked, and talked
and talked, and talked.

I do have one big regret. We didn't take the boys away from their
friends and environment often enough or in long enough periods of
time to recapture their hearts. Once Seth went on a two-week
Outward Bound-type program in Colorado that taught him some
terrific life lessons. He came home with a healthy understanding of
work, rewards and fair play, and it lasted a while. I'll never forget him
saying when I asked him to make his bed, "If you don't work, you
don't eat." He even told me that he'd quit smoking on that trip. It
was one of those honest statements that took my breath away—I had
no idea! I wish we'd been able to do more of that, take them out of
their environment more often and just play together as a family.

THE OTHER PARENTS

If the spouses, children, teachers, extended family, friends and
neighbors were all that stepfamilies had to worry about, we'd still
do pretty well. But there is at least one, and often two or more
people involved in a blended family who can throw a wrench into
stepfamily life. Being an "ex" carries a connotation just a little less
wicked than being a "step." If the stepparent isn't careful, he or she
can vent their frustrations at being prejudged as "wicked" by laying
all the blame on the spouse's "ex."

I first met the boys' mother when she and Richard were still
married. My cousin Carol and I befriended Richard in college,
and we invited him, his wife and their little boys over to dinner
one night. I remember Richard as one of those involved dads who
did diapers and crouched down to his boys' level to talk.

In college, his marriage faltered, and by the time I graduated
and moved away, he seemed destined for divorce. I had long since

pulled away from the friendship. As a single woman, I didn't want to be around for a divorced man's rebound. It was one of the smartest things I ever did. I've often felt that God rewarded me for that by bringing us together again years later.

Richard divorced, graduated and moved away to find work, only returning on occasion to see his children. Then he joined the military for the second time in his life and was stationed on the opposite side of the country from them. He didn't see the boys until we met up again and married. The last thing on earth I expected was one day to have custody of his children. They were in another state, far away. I thought we'd have our own children or adopt.

Richard did what is called the "Vanishing Father" routine.[6] Researchers have discovered that since men often deal with emotions by ignoring them, many involved fathers can't cope with losing their children, so they just leave. Out of sight, out of mind is the idea. Yet when I met Richard six years later, he was wearing a silver bracelet with the boys' initials on it. He called it a "Missing in Divorce" bracelet, like the Vietnam MIA bracelets of the '70s. He could hardly bear to see the boys, but he couldn't live a day without them.

Reappearing after a remarriage, as Richard did, is not uncommon. Other fathers take a sudden interest in children after divorce, even though they ignored them while married to their mother. These kinds of behaviors can mystify and frustrate a mother who has to deal with her children's hurt feelings and questions about Daddy.

No doubt Richard's actions, though understandable to him, were exasperating to his ex-wife. We came around years later and took an interest in the children, calling them weekly, showing concern about their schoolwork, taking them for twice-yearly visitations. This would have put new pressures on any mother or any marriage. Yet her reactions would never have pushed us into court if it weren't for the boys' stepfather. There are few excuses for disrupting a child's home.

Biological parents have to deal with tremendous emotions, guilt and anger being the most obvious. I have seen biological parents choose to misinterpret what the Other Parent said in order to keep a fight alive—as if accepting the voice of reason would be admitting defeat.

Displaced anger means being mad at one person but taking it out on another. This is typical of stepfamilies. A woman might be angry with her new husband, or with herself, but finds it easier to vent on her ex-husband. A stepfather might feel guilty about his own kids, and finds the stepchildren an available target for his frustrations. Sometimes we just have to grab hold of ourselves and stop being consumed by our own emotions!

Richard and I entered into a relationship with the Other Parents while we lived in different states, which may as well have been different planets. We had no mutual friends to serve as mediators or any mutual understandings on which to build a working relationship. It was like having the lights go out in a storm. Even though the house ought to be familiar, you still get bumped and scared as you fumble for a match. We had to deal with long-distance visitation, money and the kids' desires about where they would live.

At one point, the boys and the Other Parents moved. Because they were in another state, it was to us as if they just disappeared. This was the most frightening time of all. We tried to stay in touch with the boys' schools. Even though it was illegal for the schools to withhold information from us, we were stonewalled by a huge bias against the biological father. The school principals wouldn't even tell us if the children were alive or enrolled, so we appealed to the state capitol to try to force the situation. Schools have a natural way to win these struggles—they merely prolong compliance until the school year ends.

Although it may be *hard* to work with people we don't know and who are suspicious of us, it is not *impossible*. As Christians we have the mind of Christ. We know the will of God found in His Word. We thus have the ability to forgive, to rise above circumstances, to face pressures. We need to know that when we pray, our prayers will be heard and answered.

Within months of the boys' sudden disappearance, a lawyer was able to secure visitation for us. Within another sixty days, the courts ruled in our favor for permanent custody. We didn't seek revenge. We sought God, and He had His eyes on those kids the whole time. We just had to trust Him, keep praying and purify our hearts to see Him work.

It is ironic that spouses who divorce because they cannot get along expect to get along in determining education, money and parenting tasks related to the children. Adding to the difficulty is that often the spouses have formed relationships and marriages with other people who have their own ideas about the situation. Getting along with the Other Parents is a terrific vision that we can work and pray toward, but again, it is unrealistic to expect it to happen today.

The "can't we all just get along" attitude is unrealistic. The answer, at least at first, is, "No, we can't." Often the reason we all can't get along is simply because people have the right to exercise their own wills. Some parents have the idea that getting along means going along with *their* terms according to *their* perceptions. "If you don't play by my rules, there's gonna be a war," they seem to say. They don't have an ounce of empathy toward the Other Parents. Nor do they understand the Other Parents have their own perceptions of the situation. No one is 100 percent bad.

When I talked with my lawyer sister once about a hardship concerning visitation, Lois said, "The law protects the right of the Other Parent to be difficult." It is often gut-wrenching to live with the consequences of how other people exercise their rights, and yet even this we can do.

A proverb says, "You are a poor specimen if you cannot stand the pressure of adversity." That proverb throws down quite a challenge. The solution is to refuse to cater to our emotions and get involved in the right war! We don't wrestle against flesh and blood, but against principalities and powers.[7] The spiritual always precedes the physical. We win in the spirit realm through prayer, then the physical realm follows. As soon as we get down and dirty, wrestling with other people, we start losing because we're fighting the wrong battle.

I'm not saying we allow others to invade boundaries and manipulate us and give us avoidable grief. I'm saying that skirmishing over this little infraction and that annoying inconvenience often doesn't matter. Jesus told the storm, "Peace be still!"[8] When He faced the officials who were about to kill Him, "He kept silent and answered nothing."[9] Most things are not worth losing our peace over. We need to fight about dangerous situations but not mere inconveniences. Getting upset about who dropped off the children where or the child support check that comes a day late isn't worth making ourselves or our children miserable or causing them to feel guilty about the Other Parent. Richard went to court for his children's sake, but only after he'd already won the war in the spirit realm.

Pray and Pack

One of the primary issues in dealing with Other Parents has nothing at all to do with them. It deals with our own level of trust. Can we trust God with our children? On what basis do we trust God? Are we praying for our children? Do we know how to pray for God's protection over our children? Do we pray for the Other Parents? Have we taught our children well enough that we can trust them when they are away from us? Or do we feel the need to control every situation?

Divorced parents learn early what nondivorced parents don't have to learn until a child is eighteen—we have to trust God with our children. Divorced parents learn when the child leaves on his or her first visitation at age five or eight or thirteen. We want to protect our children, but for all children of divorce or death a part of their childhood has died as soon as that parent is gone—whether it happens at age five or eight or thirteen. A part of their innocence has been lost to them forever. Releasing our children requires facing the reality of what has happened to their young lives, releasing a false sense of control and developing trust.

Even if we can control many variables in our lives, we cannot control them all. This control issue is one of the problems in mother-dominated families. She is in charge often because she feels the need to control. If the husband gets fed up, tensions flare. Her control hurts her own kids when she can't get along with her ex-spouse. She hurts her husband too when she interjects, overshadows and corrects his every interaction with the child. Give the stepparent some tips, then let it go! The more we trust and pray, the less need we feel for control.

Trust in God is the inner well from which true faith in God flows. We can try to exercise faith, squeeze our eyes tight and recite a scripture about everything working together for the good. But if we don't have a deep well of trust and a heartfelt belief that God is working for our highest good, it's impossible to dig down, pray through, quote scriptures or believe positively and come up with a fountain of real faith.

My good friend Anna has a profound trust in God. She is able to send her teenage sons off for weeks at a time to their father who is a known womanizer and eccentric to the point of being bizarre. Nothing is bad enough to change the court-ordered visitation, so she just prays and packs.

Last summer her youngest said he wanted to move in with his dad. Anna asked him a few leading questions so he could start reasoning out why it wasn't a good idea, but he held fast. She didn't give him the satisfaction of a shocked response, nor did she change any house rules to make her home more attractive. Anna shut her mouth, packed him up for summer visitation and sent him off, praying all the way. The boy called within a week, sick and needing medical attention, but the father wouldn't hear of taking him to a doctor.

Anna took every step she could to ensure the child was taken care of, then drove him straight to a doctor when her son returned home a few weeks later, still somewhat ill. Even though the illness was not life threatening, it was a severe lesson for the child. He was cured of the illness—as well as of the bug to live with Dad. I believe God allowed that child to get a taste of what it was like to be outside the blessing of his mother's house

Anna did not exercise a blind trust, however. She made it her business to know what was happening in the Other Parent's home. Richard and I had once been more careful about emotions than welfare. To keep our kids from feeling torn between the two homes, or feeling disloyal to the custodial parents, we didn't ask them detailed questions about their home or quality of living. A psychologist was required to testify during the eventual custody hearing, and he told us that for all our good intentions, we were naïve. Parents *must* know the conditions under which their children are being raised, but we don't need to pry into the Other Parents lives needlessly, like to find out how much they earn or what they wear to work.

The Bible says, "Having done all…stand."[10] After exercising influence over our children, praying over the Other Parents and doing everything within our power to live at peace with all involved, we have to stop meddling and let God do His part. This requires letting go of control. How big is our God? We must allow God to be as big as He is and trust Him with our kids.

VISITATION WOES

Planning visitation is like getting on a freeway onramp. You know you will have to yield to the other cars, and you hope they'll let you in, but experience tells you this might be a fight and someone could get hurt.

Visitation can be as difficult as parents want to make it. By the time a divorce has occurred, so much ill-will can build up that situations become opportunities to relive the war.

One of the best solutions I have heard was about a friend who sent friendly memos through the mail to both the children and parents to confirm the arrangements of the visit. That way, if something changed, the children wouldn't blame her because they could see for themselves what had been agreed. This kept the Other Parents honest.

The best solution ever, though, is to achieve that vision where all the adults involved act like adults. I've heard of parents attending sporting events with their children, with one set of parents taking the child and the other bringing the child home. I've seen parents who are able to celebrate the child's birthday together, having one large party instead of many smaller ones for the various family factions and friends. I've even seen holidays and special events such as graduations where one set of parents hosted the Other Parents in their home. With liberal forgiveness applied, and concern concentrating on the child, this can happen, and we all know that nonwarring parents are the best parents.

Instead of this ideal, however, during visitation, children can experience anything from the extreme of possessiveness to "child dumping." In child dumping, a spouse takes the children for the weekend, but leaves them with a babysitter or grandmother or—very bad choice—with a stepmother.

I see lots of caring fathers today, although my single mom friends tell me dads are still a problem. I see fathers at the park, in stores and in restaurants, taking care of their children as a father should. Perhaps due to the emphasis on the men's movement, we'll see an end to child dumping. And, perhaps, if more fathers become involved, the cultural bias against the biological father that assumes he's the "bad guy" will begin to shift.

A possessive child is a different kind of problem, sometimes rooted in the parents. Parents who divorce make mistakes not only with their spouses, but also with their children. A boy who was given the status of becoming the "little man" while his mother was single will probably try to maintain his status, by monopolizing her time and pushing the new father aside when his mother remarries. Boys are kids, not husbands. I can also understand a girl who watched her parents divorce and her father move out now gluing herself to him whenever he is around. But girls must not be made to feel as if they are *competing* for Dad's attention or that their status as "Daddy's girl" is threatened by a grown woman.

Parents have their own issues about visitation. Stepparents do feel jealous sometimes. It is embarrassing as a grown adult to acknowledge we're jealous of a seven-year-old! We have to become so secure in ourselves and our marriage that we can weather the various phases, moods and whims we encounter. By becoming better spouses, we become better parents.

This is also true for setting house rules, which change for a child from household to household. Parents have to sit down and work it out, making an agreement with their children so the children are clear on expectations and the reasons behind them.

Few rules are unbendable. If a child is accustomed to watching a video before bedtime at home, but in your house you always read before bedtime, then sometimes it might be nice to change your rules and do what seems most natural to the child. Why be petty? If the children already living in the home know that when Elizabeth and Quinton come to visit, the children get to watch a video before bedtime, they'll look forward to these visits. Elizabeth and Quinton might otherwise seem like intruders or competitors. Sometimes to get people all working in the same direction, we just need to do what makes life fun.

If the rules of the Other Parents are abhorrent to us, we still cannot afford to attack the values of the other household. Usually differences are minor. Perhaps we eat dinner as a family around the table each night. We can't say the other family is bad, wrong, stupid or ignorant for eating in front of the television. Criticizing any parent—custodial or noncustodial—in front of a child is going to do more harm than good and will always backfire against the one who criticizes.

Money

Money, money, money. Who pays child support, and does it come on time? Often parents try to fight over this issue by using the child's visitation as collateral for extorting a check. How grievous this must be to God who has already promised to be our provider—not to mention the child who receives undue punishment as a result of his or her parents.

The rule of thumb is, don't tell children about things they have no ability to control, help or change. If a child cannot do anything about his or her parent's child support check, then the child doesn't need to know the check is late. I have a friend whose mother insisted she call her father every month to ask for the check. She still has a problem today in dealing with money. This was too much emotional responsibility to put on the shoulders of a child. Fight through with prayer in the spirit realm, then go to the courts if necessary, but don't make child support the child's fault or the child's problem or the child's punishment.

Child support was the last thing on our minds in the abrupt shift Richard and I experienced between being noncustodial parents who sent child support and had to work out visitation, to being custodial parents. But our lawyer said the courts would not approve the change unless the Other Parents paid something. The lawyers set the figure, the parents agreed and the courts approved the plan.

Money does at least two things. One, the Bible says that where our money goes, there our hearts go also.[11] It's odd that our money doesn't follow our hearts. Instead, our hearts follow our money. During those noncustodial years, it was important for me to be involved in writing out that child support check each month. By doing so, I made an investment in my stepsons' lives, and I built up an emotional bank that wanted to see a pay-off on that investment.

Allowing the Other Parents to pay does the same. It gives them legitimacy and a sense of responsibility and stewardship with their children. I have a friend who struggles financially. His ex-wife, on the other hand, married a millionaire who invested in her business, and she made another million of her own. Yet he sends her a check each month. As much of a hardship as it is, that money represents a father fulfilling his duty to his children to provide for them. Their mother can add all she wants, and that stepfather can be more of a provider dollar-for-dollar than the father, but nothing can ever change the fact that the father contributed to the best of his ability at a level that could sustain a child in a less opulent environment. It is noble to provide for our children. With our money, we send a signal and open hearts.

Richard and I decided the boys were old enough to know what we did with the checks from their mother. We figured up what we would have spent on clothes, and instead of using our money, we split the check between the boys and called it their "clothing allowance." After paying tithes, they could use the money for legitimate expenses under our guidance. This thrilled them. They knew it came from their mother, they knew we were fair with it, and more than anything, they had their own money to spend. The first time Seth got his he was so excited he ironed it, making crisp, flat bills.

The results were mixed, but always satisfactory. Josh became a clotheshorse. Instead of going to a discount house to buy lots of things, he would invest in one expensive item each month. He also spent it the moment he received it, then waited for the next month to roll around. Seth made his money stretch further and spent it slower. He wanted music lessons, which we couldn't afford, so he used some of his money for lessons and spent the rest on inexpensive clothes.

In later years, the boys moved around, and all the adults dropped the issue of child support. We had far greater problems to tackle. But for those first few years, the boys' mother was meticulous about sending the checks. Whether anyone was aware of it, this kept an open door for a continued relationship between them.

On the other hand, money is one of the most contentious issues in human life. Married people fight over money and children. In a stepfamily, these subjects often intensify. Children are expensive! I'll never forget noticing one morning as I was leaving for work after the boys moved in that there were seven empty milk jugs in the recycle bin, which was sitting out for pick up. Seven! I figured up what they cost, multiplied it by the number of weeks and realized I was making $35 per month in milk payments!

Then there were school supplies. We joined the crowds of parents who were wrestling around in the aisles of the local discount store trying to match dwindling stacks of supplies with the items listed on pieces of paper we received from each class. By the time we went through the checkout line, I felt as if I'd bought supplies for the entire seventh grade. Then two weeks later the kids were asking to borrow a pen.

Richard and I became expert economizers, although bargain shopping to us is nothing like the sport it is to many of our friends. My spending habits changed overnight when the boys came. You can have kids or clothes—not both. I struggled to make adjustments. Once made, the amount of money we had seemed "normal."

If we have it in our hearts to be resentful, angry and petty, there is no end to the things we can find in life on which to fasten our irritation. Spending money on children lasts only for a season, then our lives move on, and the children are gone. As shocking as it is to spend that money, and as much as we might want to spend it elsewhere, it's just not worth losing our peace over.

God's provision exceeds abundantly above anything we can ask or think. We can trust Him to make money stretch to cover our needs today. We can believe He will give us the desires of our hearts tomorrow.

MOVING IN

Christ's disciples came up with what they thought was a great solution when they were faced with a hungry mob of people. A crowd had just listened to Jesus, and the people were famished. The disciple's solution was easy: "Send them away!" We all at times tend to think, *Hey, I know! Get rid of the people, and we won't have a problem!*

A proverb states that an empty stable stays clean, but you can't make money off an empty stable. Applied to business, this means that without employees you won't have the hassles of management, but you also won't be able to make money. In the home, this means that if you don't have kids, all these child-rearing problems will disappear, as will many of the problems in the marriage that stem from child rearing. But without children, you also won't have a family.

What's the solution? When the disciples questioned Jesus about the hungry crowd, He said, "Feed them." Then He took what He had, blessed it and started giving it away. That was when the miracle took place.

Tommy Barnett wrote a book called *There's a Miracle in Your House* about starting where you are with what you have. "Inside every human being is a miracle waiting to be discovered and released," he wrote.[12] An old classic called *Acres of Diamonds* tells that the idea for riches is right in your backyard. You just have to find it.

It's easy to say when children act out that they'd be better off with someone else. Our society is like that. We've passed our problems off to the government, churches, schools and corporations as if it is their duty to fix us. Agencies and companies can help, but the primary unit of society is the family. We have to be part of the solution, if not the whole solution. The answer for our kids is in our own homes.

Many times I wanted to throw in the towel. "Weary of well-doing," I wanted to quit giving, quit believing, quit dealing. In addition to outward disruptions, tremendous energies surged inside each of us to re-create our environment into something recognizable. Each of us wanted that emotional "comfort zone" that felt like our own idea of home and family. Conflicts arose because we each came from different backgrounds.

If people marry who have grown up together and shared the same values, then remarry people from that same crowd, chances are the children each family inherits in the divorce will have similar feelings about what constitutes a home. But in our diverse culture and transient society, more people may find themselves in the situation Richard and I found. We were different.

CAN STEPFAMILIES BE DONE RIGHT?

I had grown up on church pews, had a minister for a father and had not one single divorce in my entire family tree. I married a man whose parents divorced when he was ten. Although his father has been sober now for more than thirty years, he had been an alcoholic. Richard and I did well in communicating and dealing with day-to-day living, but his idea of "family" came from what he studied in books. He didn't know the "family feeling" I had. As one researcher puts it, I had been to "marriage school" by watching my parents.[13] Richard hadn't.

The kids, on the other hand, were accustomed to chaos—self-imposed, self-inflicted chaos.

At one time, I read a book on sexual addiction that claimed that much of the sex addict's drive comes from the desire to have a rush of adrenaline in his or her system. The longer the addict is in a behavior, the more it takes for that adrenaline to get working, which is why the addict is always looking for a bigger thrill. In other words, it's like a chemical addiction.

Although I have never seen a study about this, I felt that my children were, in a similar way, addicted to their own adrenaline. They couldn't tolerate peace. Whenever we had a peaceful day, I could set my watch, knowing that by noon the next day, some explosion would occur. They had a "need" of some kind to make our home into what felt comfortable, which was not a place where they would be nurtured by two loving parents. Peace felt uncomfortable to them.

Every family has "ghosts" that come with it. Richard brought his parents, I brought mine. And the kids brought the Other Parents. At times I felt like my husband and kids were crazy. But I added my own "craziness" by striving to create a "normal" family that looked like one in which the parents had been married for twenty years and planned and birthed these children together. It was just not going to happen. In that sense, we all were "crazy."

To try to force a stepfamily to act like a nuclear family is to force a disaster.

Sending the children to live with someone else would take away the burr under the saddle, but it wouldn't remove the saddle itself. Richard and I had issues to deal with in our own lives and between ourselves. Having his children in our home brought these issues to the surface. Getting rid of the kids would not solve anything.

Bringing noncustodial kids into the home may also not resolve anything. With all the emotions parents feel about raising their children with a nonbiological parent or raising someone else's children or leaving their children to be raised by someone else, it's only natural that parents sometimes goof up. Some parents look for opportunities with nonresident kids to lure them into their homes. Some fathers who carry guilt about their divorce want to "make it up" to the kids by having the children live with them.

A father might also feel left out of the relationship his new wife has with her child. Instead of looking for ways to be included in their lives, he might want to even the score by having his biological child in the home as well.

One friend of mine acted on these emotions and became convinced his preteen son wanted to move in with him. In the custody hearing, the child said he wanted to stay with his mother. He had only told his dad he wanted to live with him to make his dad feel better. What a blow—and costly, too. Children want to please parents, so it is crucial that parents find a way to determine if a child is serious about moving. One way is to bring in professional or pastoral help.

The only reasons for taking a child from the resident family is if the child is endangered or if the child insists on leaving and is of an age to choose. It is not unusual for young teens to move in with their noncustodial parent, generally the father. It is also not unusual for this decision to break a mother's heart.

CAN STEPFAMILIES BE DONE RIGHT?

The bottom line is this: Sending the child away is not the best solution, regardless of how crazy we feel. Cashing in a child's unhappiness and luring a child out of his or her custodial parent's home is also no solution. However, if a teenager wants to move, it is probably the *only* solution.

THE GREAT MISTAKE

My biggest mistake came straight out of these emotional complexities involved in stepfamily life. The literature tells us that it is important for a child to continue having a relationship with the noncustodial parent and extended family. Stepparents and biological parents do not serve their children well if they try to cut off part of the family for spite or any other reason. After all, the stepparent is not the biological parent and never will be.

Every child has a link to his or her biological parents. Even abused children who are placed into foster homes are excited when a parent comes to see them. They long to please the parent, to believe the parent, even if that parent is a drug addict who makes empty promises.

My big mistake was that I didn't see the emotional turmoil my children had about their mother's household. I didn't understand—wasn't there to see—the relationship they'd had with their stepfather. I had a full-blown case of "can't we all just get along," and I wanted my kids to stay in touch with the Other Parents for the noblest of reasons. In 99 percent of stepfamilies, the child's relationship with the Other Parent is crucial. But in our family, my children had too many unresolved feelings and memories that had not yet been dealt with from their childhood.

I kept at the same mistake for years. Richard had been divorced from his ex-wife's entire family, not just his ex-wife, so I think he agreed with me and blamed any misgivings he might have on the emotions he had from a decade earlier. On family vacations, we often ended up near the mother's extended family, so we always went out of our way to ensure the boys saw their maternal grandparents, aunts, uncles and cousins. I also encouraged the boys to call and talk to them on holidays. I always reminded the boys of their mother's birthday, Mother's Day and made sure they had help to send Christmas cards or gifts. If they didn't respond, I sometimes pushed it, making sure the card was sent or the call was made. I didn't understand that my actions hit my kids' with an emotional bump and that I put them in a tailspin they were too young to understand, much less handle.

Some years after this came to a head, a friend told me her experience, and I started to understand what I'd done. My friend was adopted as a baby from an American Indian reservation. She was twelve years old when her adoptive mother was having difficulty with her. My friend seemed to be pulling away from her adoptive family. Her mother felt my friend wanted to be able to express more of who she was as a Native American. The mother misread the daughter's need for identity and believed that her breaking away came out of a need to find her "roots."

The mother took the girl to the reservation to show her where she came from. This was a very traumatic experience for the young girl. She was unable to distinguish her own feelings, much less articulate them. But later as an adult she recognized that as a result of that trip to the reservation she had felt a huge rejection. She felt as if her mother had been rubbing in her face the fact that she wasn't part of the family after all—that she didn't "fit in."

I feel I did the same thing with our boys. Just when the kids were settling into life with us, a holiday or birthday would come up, and I would again remind them they weren't mine. In our home, which should have been a safe haven, I was nagging Seth to remember his mother and stepfather, about whom he felt

117

ambivalent. It came across not just as an emotional bump, but as a jolt, a scream, "WE ARE NOT A REAL FAMILY!"

At the same time, Seth's emotional condition was changing. He had been like a giant iceberg, but he was was now melting under the blowtorch of our love and a nurturing family life. I didn't see when he liquified and was able to start feeling again. I never noticed the difference in him. The result was a disaster.

Just as Seth was getting in touch with his emotions, his hormones were kicking in, and a natural desire for separation from us occurred. At the same time, he was hanging around with one boy—and maybe many friends—who had problems with step-parents. These friendships influenced him. It was like pouring fuel into a Molotov cocktail. Just when our stepfamily should have been calming into a routine, this bottle called Seth was being shaken and was sure to explode.

SETH— I remember when my stepmom helped Josh and me decorate our rooms. I liked how she let us pick our own color schemes and paint our dressers. It was fun. We seemed so unified in doing that kind of stuff. I never put together many projects before then, but accomplishing something together helped build our relationship. We made a good team, and I was aware of that at the time. I also liked that I saw her spend money on us to help make our rooms comfortable.

Money was a huge value to me as a child even though I didn't understand how it worked or where it came from. The first thing I ever learned about money was that where our treasure is, our heart goes. My parents may not have thought I was listening, but I learned that principle in my early teens. Since then, I've put that principle into practice in many ways. For example, if my girlfriend wanted me to do something that I didn't want to do, I would pay for it so I would be committed to it. I'm now careful of where my money goes because I watch where my heart will follow.

For that same reason, my parents always told me they wouldn't buy me a car. They said that if I didn't pay for it, I wouldn't value it. The most they would do was meet us halfway if we saved up enough to pay cash. Josh and I didn't expect a car, but we were still disappointed as we grew up when we saw other kids get theirs. Today, I agree with my parents on that. Every kid I knew who was given a car by his or her parents wrecked them. So I've totally adopted the policy my parents had.

Family was something I valued, but only in part. Because of the size and variety of my extended family, I grew up under the influence of lots of different people and ideas. I have uncles who play music, sing, deejay, produce videos, run restaurants and sell. I have aunts who sing, practice law and decorate, and grandparents who love sports, nature and God. And I have cousins who are good friends. I look back at family times throughout my life, and they always were exciting.

My stepmom refers to a stepfamily tree as a "hedgerow," but to me it feels more like a "forest." It's good to know that I can get a change of pace by visiting family somewhere and that they're spread all over the country. I'm interested in travel and people, so getting to know them all in the different lives they live would be fun, and I could learn from each of them. The only bad part is that I didn't develop deep relationships with any of my extended family. I know they are there pulling for me, and if the family has a problem, I'll rally with the rest of them, but I don't know them well from spending time with them regularly.

Friends, on the other hand, are a whole different story. From my perspective, friends had nothing to do with any member of my family. Just me. I chose who to spend my time with at school and who I would hang out with after school. I never chose to hang out with kids who went home after school and spent time with their parents. I didn't much like kids who talked about family things they did or how cool their dads were. I pretty much thought that well-adjusted, happy-go-lucky kids were dorks.

I was drawn to kids who had the same attitude I had. I liked the kids who caused trouble. I thought the cool kids were the kids who had no problem with breaking the rules, and in fact were courageous about it. My theory back then was that kids who often broke the rules—problem kids—were the free thinkers, the nonconformists who made decisions for themselves. It wasn't until I was older that I realized I liked creative types who looked for unique ways of doing things and saw the world "outside the box" of conventional thinking. At the time I just knew I was drawn to problem kids who might have been creative and didn't know how to express themselves in productive ways. Or kids who were just rebels. Either kind was fine with me.

Much of who I became when I was young was due to the people I chose to spend my time with—the people with whom I shared my thoughts and ideas. My friends weren't to blame for all the wrong decisions I made in my life. That's where parents get it wrong, thinking that if it weren't for peer pressure, little Johnny would be perfect. Peer pressure is a two-way street—together we all influenced one another in bad ways. The atmosphere in which my friends lived and that we encouraged one another to be a part of shaped a lot of my character. It led me to lots of wrong choices.

My friend Chris and I went to school together only in the eighth grade. We had gone to different middle schools, so we didn't know each other until that year when a new junior high opened. We both started school with rebellious reputations from the middle schools from which we came. Instead of going head to head to determine who was craziest, we just ran together. We played off one another.

I remember that Chris did have a very bad attitude about his stepfather, which contributed to my dislike for my stepmother.

We contributed to each other's rebellion. We even had plans to run away from home and take off for California together. He wound up bailing out on that idea while I waited up all night for him to pick me up. He never came.

Being around Chris really did convince me that I hated my stepmom as much as he hated his stepdad. The two households in which we lived were completely different. I'm positive that if he had lived in my place, he would be here now writing this book. Instead, the last I saw him about three years ago, he was a heroin addict who had the same bad attitude he had in middle school.

I had always looked up to Chris. I thought he was funnier, better looking and all-around cooler than I was. I aspired to be as cool as he was. I almost replaced the codependent relationship with my brother due to Chris's friendship. That's how much his friendship meant to me.

When I started ninth grade, everything changed—including my friendship with Chris. At school, I started hanging out with Chris as usual. There was this girl, Sarah, who Chris really wanted to date that year. We found out that she liked one of us, but we weren't sure who it was. In one of those schoolyard romance things, she said she'd have a friend let us know which one of us she wanted to meet at her locker after school.

I knew I wasn't as cool as Chris, so I knew it was him. I remember the look on Chris's face when we found out she liked me. I think that he was even more surprised than I was. We didn't hang out much after that except on rare occasions, partly because of the girl, but even more because I had to transfer schools. I had destroyed school property, and the school I attended was going to suspend me. I wound up going to a private school. It was not a good way to start the year.

The other problem relationship I had was with my biological mother. I didn't think about her **much**. I never wrote, called or initiated any type of communication except at the request of my stepmom. At Mother's Day, I thought of my *stepmom*, not my *mom*. It was probably due to a combination of fear, hurt, betrayal and guilt that kept me from wanting to think about my biological mom. I feared she would be angry and not want a relationship with me. I felt hurt because I was away from her. I felt betrayed because all the years I grew up I never knew that I was being wronged. I felt guilty because I left her and moved in with my dad. At that time she despised him.

I had always been very confused about what had happened with the court case and how I felt about the parents I left behind. Sometimes I hated life. Other times I just didn't understand what was wrong, why I had moved. It was hard to think about leaving my mother. It was painful to think that she was somewhere having a life with my little sister and without me because I left her. I loved, and still love, my mom, and I don't want to know that she is hurting, especially if it involves me.

My stepmother encouraged me to pursue a relationship with my mother, and she's probably right that it stretched my loyalties and left me even more confused. It was one thing—actually a good thing—to allow me to have a relationship with my mother. But it was another thing to try and impose that relationship on me when I couldn't handle it. That turned into a bad thing.

Sometimes I feel my emotional life is a warmed-over battlefield. I still have things I haven't dealt with, even though I'm an "adult" now. I do know for a fact, however, that the people I choose to make a part of my life are directly related to the results I produce in my life. I understand now not to underestimate the power and negative influence that people can have. If I were to give one word of advice to stepkids reading this, or anyone for that matter, it would be, "Do not be misled: 'Bad company corrupts good character.'"[14]

5

THERE ARE HOLES IN ALL THE DOORS

JOANN— THUMP! THUMP! I will never forget the sound of boys fighting or the feeling of the upstairs floor shaking under my feet, windows rattling, sometimes furniture falling. Every morning I tried to get my prayer time and a shower in before the boys woke up. If I didn't—Lord! I'd wake them up after my devotions, hop in the shower and within minutes I could feel in my feet the thuds of bodies landing elsewhere upstairs. I never got out of the shower fast enough to find out what it was all about, and I never understood how anyone could get in a fight within the first few minutes of waking up in the morning. But these kids were always ready. Every day.

As much as I wanted to scream at them to get an immediate result, I had to concentrate on the fact that discipline was about shaping them, not about making my life easier. *The fact that a well-disciplined child is a joy to his or her parents is secondary. The first priority is the development of the child.*

CAN STEPFAMILIES BE DONE RIGHT?

One of the elements in great leadership is to concentrate on principles and strategies that will achieve long-term goals, rather than settling for a quick fix. Disciplining a child to become a capable, competent person is one of the parent's greatest tasks, and if the stepparents have signed on to help, this includes them. Yet discipline is the number one cause of disagreement in a step-family.[1]

"Every human being is born on our planet with the potential to become capable, not with the capabilities themselves," Dr. H. Stephen Glenn wrote.[2] His studies from hundreds of sources led him to derive seven characteristics that children must develop to become healthy, well-adjusted citizens.

1. *Children need the confidence that they have personal capabilities and the ability to learn and grow.* Richard and I had to reinforce continually to Josh and Seth that they would progress by using their own abilities, not by our pushing them or by accident. Sometimes the way we reinforced this was by letting go of situations, which sends a clear message that we think they are capable of finding their own way.

2. *Children should be loved, respected and needed in the family.* Every day we had to point out to the boys that they mattered to the whole family. They weren't remote islands. They needed to understand their lives had meaning and purpose.

3. *The child is not a victim, but has influence over the outcome of his or her own life.* Seth believed he was tossed about by circumstances and a "fate" over which he had no control. This contributed to the anger he felt but repressed. Our job was to teach him cause and effect, that he had the power to put things in motion, then reap the rewards or suffer the consequences.

4. *Children need the skill of self-discipline—the ability to understand personal thoughts and emotions and to develop self-control and self-discipline.*

5. *Children must learn to communicate.*

6. *Children must learn and practice personal and social responsibility.*

7. *Children need to learn to make decisions based on good values and principles.[3]*

DARE TO DISCIPLINE

At the same time Dr. Glenn was developing his thesis, Dr. James Dobson was teaching Christian parents what the Bible said about discipline. Discipline had become distorted and perverted, and Dr. Dobson brought it back to the forefront. My beat-up copy of his landmark book, *Dare to Discipline,* is dated 1974, which is the year I first heard him speak.[4] Dr. Dobson's premise is that discipline flows from the respect children have toward their parents or authorities. From that point, discipline can take several forms, depending on the child. The first problem for stepparents is to gain respect.

Seth had played the role of the "scapegoat" in his original family. That means he would bring attention to himself by acting out in negative ways in order to keep the family from facing what was really wrong, which in his case was his stepfather's problems. He brought this habit into our home, even though the stepfather had been left behind.

Besides that, Josh and Seth had adopted a "survivor" mentality, and they were codependent. Josh was the manipulator. Seth allowed himself to be manipulated and got angry about it, but if anyone stepped in, he covered up for both of them. Getting through to them was like moonwalking toward a goal. You put out a lot of effort, and it looks like you're going forward, but you're slipping further and further away.

Between them, they expended tremendous energy in trying to re-create their old home in ours. They had a habit of dysfunctional behavior, and even though it was bad for them and they knew it was bad, it was the only life they knew. Subconsciously they clung to their old ways as a place of comfort. As a result, I felt tremendous underlying pressures to become someone I wasn't. It was subtle, but in essence, they were trying to force me to become their stepfather.

The first time I ever yelled at my kids made an indelible impression on me. I couldn't believe what I'd done. They didn't even notice. They had been left home on a summer morning until Richard or I could leave work to go take them somewhere. For some reason, we had a big shoebox of pennies at the time, and we used them for various games. Who knows why families end up with weird things like shoeboxes of pennies, but anyway that's what we had.

I walked into the house, and the boys were in a penny fight in the living room, one on the couch using the back of the couch as a shield, the other behind the couch in another part of the room, right in front of a freshly-painted wall. Pennies were flying, chinking against the wall, clinking against furniture, and the boys were yelling and laughing.

At first I said, "What are you doing?" They glanced at me, then kept throwing and fighting. I repeated myself, and this time they ignored me. I yelled, "STOP IT RIGHT NOW!" When I started toward them and yelled it again, they stopped. I had never been around kids who didn't respond to an adult entering a room. I couldn't understand what on earth they were thinking. That's before I discovered they *weren't* thinking, just reacting.

126

There Are Holes in All the Doors

By the time I yelled the second time, I was shaking. I had never imagined myself being a screamer and couldn't reconcile the calm person I thought I was on the inside with what I had just done on the outside. I had come from the "Nancy Cole school of parenting." My mom was so kind, understanding and gracious that she was a wonder to all my friends. We all obeyed her, as I recall it, but she never raised a voice or a finger.

Mom would say things like, "I wish you wouldn't load the dishwasher that way." "Joann, why don't you get the living room vacuumed today?" "Girls, I'd like your room picked up by noon." These requests and wishes were respected, and we did as was insinuated we ought to do. Even my kids obeyed my mother's wishes and requests as if they were demands and orders. How she did it, in part, was that my dad was always behind her watching if anyone didn't do as she only hoped they might. Even without him around, she was so nice, even strangers catered to her.

That was my experience with motherhood. On the other hand, I always admired those mothers who take on the whole world. They not only tell their children what to do in no uncertain terms, but they also direct their children's friends, the neighbors, the kids hanging out down on the corner. My friend Karen is like that. Even living in New York City, I doubt she'd think twice about demanding of a teenager walking down the street at night, "Does your mama know where you are?" I'd be hiding in the car with the windows up and doors locked!

I discovered I was neither of these kinds of mothers. As one friend put it, I hadn't developed my maternal authority by the time the kids arrived. New parents have time to adjust to children. Their babies and toddlers don't even notice the mistakes the parent is making. But I was just there, with everyone looking at me, and I couldn't figure out what to do. I was also in limbo about what authority I had the right to exert over my boys.

over the kids

CAN STEPFAMILIES BE DONE RIGHT?

Dr. Bray says that four "tasks" must be accomplished by blended families. The family has to resolve how they will parent, manage change, separate a second marriage from the first and deal with the nonresidential parent.[5]

More than half of stepfamily marriages fail, and most of those fail within the first two years. These four tasks are often the culprits. People with idealistic notions of stepfamily life have the highest failure rate. But it's the parents who determine if a family will succeed or fail, not the children. Richard and I had committed ourselves to each other for life, and nothing the boys did was going to change that. We held fast, and they had to comply—or leave. With our commitment to each other intact, we set about figuring out a way to parent them.

For me, it all boiled down to the fact that children belong to the biological parents. Stepparents have to respect that and find a way to fit in, to strike a balance they can live with that is amenable to the Other Parent and also acceptable to the children. What we decided was that Richard would set all the rules. I was just one of the enforcers. The kids didn't like that role, nor did they respect it right away, but I wasn't there to win a Mrs. Mom contest. I had signed on for life.

Her rules are ignored - she isn't respected

Richard is a military man—self-disciplined, fit and trim, never late. But he did not bring a hint of military discipline into our home. He was not authoritarian with the boys. He instituted clear-cut rules, set consequences for infractions, then let the boys learn to operate within the structure. *we can't even Get kids to bed or To Appointments on Time!*

I want →

It took tremendous self-discipline on our parts to stick with this. We also held two convictions that were sort of rules for ourselves. One was to be consistent. Richard was reasonable, but he wouldn't budge on basics. He wouldn't create rules for special circumstances, and even though we changed consequences so we could discover things that worked, he didn't increase consequences for

If something isn't working, I Take over - Have to Fix it

128

behavior that was worse than we'd expected. Whatever he said he was going to do, he did.

The other was that we would not strike our boys. It would have been demoralizing to their burgeoning manhood, destructive to any respect for us that may have been growing—and since both boys seemed impervious to pain, I think they would have become more defiant, not less so. I also think any kind of physical punishment would have given the boys the excuse to defy all authority because of their belief that "all parents are alike." Richard is a big, intimidating man, and I'm sure just his presence, or just his looking like he could hit them, was scary enough for them.

After ~~Richard~~ *we* set simple, clear rules, we hung on for the ride. The boys would either live by what ~~Richard~~ decreed, or they wouldn't. Richard's feeling was that if they didn't, that was their choice, and ~~he~~ *we* would just let them suffer whatever predetermined or natural consequences occurred.

The only problem was that this drove me crazy! Sometimes I didn't want these kids disciplined, I wanted them *punished!* I'm emotional, confrontational and goal-oriented. I wanted to see results—*now.* Yet I also tend to be a rescuer, which makes me a prime candidate to serve as an "enabler" in a dysfunctional family system. Richard had to balance me, or I could have hopped on the roller coaster the boys created and helped it pitch and roll.

On the other hand, Richard was sometimes unfair. He would take up for the boys against me right in front of them. In later years I discovered the boys had recognized this and knew it was unfair. This was still a mistake on his part, because it slowed the boys' development of respect for me. But I couldn't change that because Richard couldn't see it. It was like asking the boys to mop the kitchen floor. Their eyes could not see dirt so they would get it wet, not clean. That was the only chore I couldn't give them. I mopped the floor myself. With Richard, I would talk about his unfairness, but I could not force him to change what his eyes could not see. Eleven years after the boys came to live with us, the day came that he saw it.

"I do that?" he asked. He had never heard me, nor seen his own actions, nor felt himself doing it. It was like a "biological parent filter" that worked like the boys' "dirt filter."

Instead of fighting what I could not change, I satisfied myself during those times with counting backward from eighteen. It doesn't take stepparents two seconds to add up the years, months and maybe even days—depending on how frustrated we are—until the child reaches an age when we are no longer responsible. I didn't do it every day, but in bad times I calculated where we were with Seth on the eighteen-year scale.

Yet even when I was forced into a backseat about discipline, I continued to exercise influence. I learned this from my friend Mary Jean Pidgeon. In a bygone era, mothers nurtured their children, and fathers administered discipline, but the mother's role was no less powerful than the father's. The saying goes, "The hand that rocks the cradle rules the world." *The stepparent can choose to exercise the power of influence, which is as great as the power of discipline.*

Overall, Richard and I presented a united front to the boys. Regardless of how I felt, I didn't change or bend the rules. If Richard said it, that's what we did. If the kids or I wanted to petition the rule, then we'd approach Richard on it, and he became the authority. This worked well for us overall. Richard never had to wonder what I was doing with the kids out of his presence. The kids never felt like I was an interloper, impinging on their happiness by setting down unfair rules just to restrain them. I never had to be the "bad guy."

It sounds simple. But was it ever hard!

DESTRUCTIVE VALUES

Once again, the boys' values played into how we operated as a family. One "value" dear to their hearts was defying and even mocking authority. I'll never forget when our care group was in our home one summer Sunday evening, and the boys went outdoors with the other children. A ruckus interrupted us, and all the adults filed outside to see what happened. Seems my kids had been teaching the pastors' children how to throw rocks at cars in order to get people angry enough to get out and chase them.

I remember even after Josh was old enough to have grown out of this stage, he remained stuck in it. One afternoon as I drove him home from a private school he attended for a short time, I overheard a humorous, yet sad conversation. Riding in the back with Josh was a boy who had just stopped homeschooling to attend this school. Josh was regaling him with all the "fun" things he used to do, like getting cops to chase him. The boy couldn't understand what Josh was saying. "You mean, you *tried* to get cops to chase you?"

"Yeah!"

"Why?"

"Why? What do you mean why? Because it's fun, man. It's great!"

The friendship didn't last, nor did Josh last at that school. I tried to talk to Josh about why such behavior made no sense to the boy or to me, but he wanted to believe it was fun, and I couldn't dissuade him.

Josh and Seth also seemed to enjoy fighting. I'm sure it provided a release from the anger they felt about other things. Whatever the cause was, the outcome was that they fought.

I raced home every day before the kids arrived from school when they first came to live with us. I worked for my brother, and he allowed me to change my schedule to accommodate my instant family. For a while, I even moved my office home and worked from the living room. That was good for me and for them. But I remember one day getting home a little late and finding the boys already home—and already fighting.

I walked in the house just in time to see Josh sprint down the stairs as Seth bellowed curses I didn't realize he knew. I ran up to the landing and saw Seth, his neck enlarged, popping with veins and reddened, his eyes red-rimmed, his hair tussled, his fists clenched and his body taut with anger. I don't know what went through my mind first, but I know the second thought was, "You poor thing!"

It's not safe to get in the middle of two animals who are trying to fight, but I grabbed Seth into an instinctive hug. He allowed me to hold him.

"I love you, Seth," I said. "Everything's going to be OK."

"It wasn't my fault, Mom!" Josh started yelling up from the bottom of the stairs.

"Josh, go away!" I said.

Josh rarely obeyed a word I said, and this was no exception. But I tuned him out while I just hugged Seth. What a pitiful little struggling creature. He had looked like a male cat that tries to puff up his body to look bigger in preparation for a fight. How horrid for a boy of twelve to feel the need for such a thing. My hug seemed to calm Seth, and when I felt his body start to relax, I let go. Then we tried to figure out what happened.

We got to the bottom of it, finding that Josh and Seth had fought over the telephone in Seth's room. Why that made sense to them, I'll never know, since they both had telephones in their rooms—until that day. As they fought for the phone, Josh had hit Seth in the head with it. That's what triggered Seth's rage. But I would soon learn this was a mild form of anger for Seth.

Seth's repertoire of emotions was limited to two. If he wasn't funny and happy, he was angry. Seth didn't know how to be embarrassed, hurt, fearful, disappointed, anxious or any of the normal range of negative, uncomfortable emotions that most people take in stride during the course of a day. If Seth wasn't happy, he was angry. And when he was angry, he was fighting mad.

Seth would often fight for no apparent reason. As time went on, I saw something of a pattern—most of the time when Seth fought, the fight happened when he was tired. Since he didn't know how to feel or interpret feelings, when he was irritable, he just became angry and thought it was justified. After I figured it out, I started warning him on the day after he spent the night at someone else's house or stayed up late at ours. I remember going through it one morning before school.

"Seth, you're tired today, and when you're tired you know what happens."

"I get in a fight."

"That's right. So just remember when you get annoyed that it's not as big a deal as it seems."

It didn't quite do the trick, and Richard and I were called down to a meeting with the principal later to hear what had happened. Seth had slugged a bigger kid as he passed him in the hallway right in front of the principal's office. The man had a floor-to-ceiling wall of glass separating his office from the main thoroughfare where kids passed one another between classes.

"Look out this window!" the principal said. "He was right there! Right in front of me! And he still punched him!"

The principal had to tell us why he was expelling Seth for a day, although he had genuine admiration for Seth's pluck, willingness to tell the truth and calm acceptance of discipline. At home, we learned that Seth and the boy had been quarreling about a girl. When they passed in the hallway, the boy purposely bumped Seth's shoulder. Seth spun, slugged him in the stomach to make him double over low enough so Seth could land a blow to his chin. It cost Seth a day of school, which meant for us another day of hassle and taking time off work.

This was how it went. When they weren't innovative and wonderful, attending concerts, writing thank-you notes and watching classic movies with me, Josh and Seth practiced open, outright rebellion. They weren't sullen or sneaky or withdrawn. They were gregarious, and invited all their friends to join in the rebellion.

One year on the day after Thanksgiving, Richard and I had invited singles and other displaced persons to our house for a day-after-Thanksgiving feast. We'd had a great day, and some of the group had gone outside to play basketball as most everyone else was leaving. Seth was hit in the head on the court and stalked into the house, slamming his bedroom door behind him.

This time his injury was combined with humiliation, and it triggered what I'd call his severe anger. He was prone at those times to lock his door, take off all his clothes and slip between the cool sheets of his bed where nothing could touch or irritate him. He would lay there for hours like that, without ever unwinding, relaxing or sleeping. During his severest times of anger, Richard would go check on him in the middle of the night, and Seth would still be lying there on his back, staring up at the ceiling, expressionless, motionless. Richard often spent the night on the spare bed in Seth's room on those occasions, in silent support of his child.

On this particular occasion, we had been planning to go to the movies after most of the people left. My friend Camella was waiting on me downstairs, and Josh met me in the upstairs hallway, right in front of Seth's bedroom door.

"Are we going to the movies?" Josh asked.

"I think you and Seth will stay home with Dad while Camella and I go," I said.

"Seth always ruins everything for us," Josh whined.

I knew Josh wasn't innocent in what happened to Seth on the court, and it triggered my anger. But I had my bright green piece of paper on my refrigerator door, and I was well-rehearsed in what we were doing as a family.

"Josh, in this family we will love one another, no matter what happens. We will accept one another. We will respect one another. And your brother needs time to cool down, so we'll let it go at that!"

Beaten, Josh asked, "Well, if he starts feeling better can we go?"

"Yes, Dad knows where we'll be, and you guys will meet us there."

Richard showed up at the theatre with both boys, and I hugged Seth and told him I hoped he was feeling better. Later Richard told me that Josh had come downstairs when I did and watched television until Seth showed up without explanation, asking if it were too late to go to the movies.

We never knew what Seth was going through or how he interpreted the world through the warped impressions of life he held. All we knew was that we were dealing with a time bomb that had to be diffused somehow through some miracle of God's grace, or it would explode. "He who is often rebuked, and hardens his neck, will suddenly be destroyed, and that without remedy" is the way the Bible puts it.[6]

It's a pretty sorry state of affairs when the closest you can get to your child is to hug him as he's in a rage or stick up for him when he's so enraged he's immobilized. But as sick as this might sound, those were victories to me—the times I got to love as much as I wanted; the times Seth let me pour a soothing balm on his troubled little soul; the times I felt like I had something to offer, if only an understanding heart or a hug.

I would complain about their fighting sometimes, but other

people would just smile and say, "Boys will be boys." Yes, boys fight. But my kids were *all* fight.

I prayed for them, tried to do my part and waited for a miracle. One day I got to witness something close to it. I saw a light go on, as if a light bulb appeared over the tops of both of their heads. Josh was sixteen and driving the family car for prearranged and approved outings. This day they'd gone to a Texas Rangers baseball game where they met up with some friends they'd just met.

They always met people—and Josh always met girls. Whether alone or together, they were always the social ones, the life of the party, the center of social activities at summer camps, the boys most of the other kids looked up to. A trip to the ballgame with new friends sounded like a normal, healthy thing for them to do, and we gave them the car keys with our blessings and with a sigh of relief that we'd have an afternoon to ourselves.

The next day, they sat at the kitchen table across from each other eating lunch and talking about the game. I was folding laundry, which I'd heaped in the chair at the end of the table, and I encouraged them to talk. I have no idea if they ever saw the ballgame, but they were full of what happened in the stands. It seems one of the girls with whom they were friends had several other friends at the game, one of whom was a teenage boy.

"Did you see him looking at us?" Seth said.

"It's OK, I could have taken him," Josh said.

"Yeah, well you pretty much tried to, except he didn't want to fight."

"Maybe he was too chicken. He might have thought it was two against one, so he better not try."

Silence as they pondered the oddity of a kid who wouldn't fight them.

"Maybe he didn't want to fight at all," I suggested.

"Yeah," Josh said, perking up and looking at Seth as if I didn't exist. "Maybe that kid wasn't looking at us to fight us."

"Maybe he was just looking at us because he didn't know us," Seth said.

"Maybe he didn't want to fight us, but we wanted to fight him, just because we thought he wanted to fight us."

"Maybe we always think people want to fight us, but they don't really want to fight us, and we just think that because we want to fight them!" Seth said.

"Yeah! I think you're right!" Josh said. He jumped up and held his hand high in the air.

"Hey, we figured something out!" Seth said, standing to slap a high five.

The sudden brainstorm died down, and they fell to eating again, but my heart was beating and my mind was soaring. Wow! They figured out that not everyone in this world likes or needs to fight.

Their negative behavior continued, as well as the small victories. They played soccer. Josh played softball. Seth wrestled. We helped one another clean the house. Whenever we saw one another, said good-bye or talked on the telephone, we'd say, "I love you." Josh was always doing, planning, going, organizing, getting his next day under way before it was night. Seth was always funny, able to crack jokes witty enough for adults. And drawing, drawing, drawing.

A general belief is that stepchild rebellion stems from unresolved feelings about the divorce. But Seth had been a baby, and had only known his biological mother and stepfather's home, then ours. He was the product of not one, but two blended families. He would never know a nuclear family until he started one himself.

I wondered if perhaps they were mad at Richard deep inside because they felt he had abandoned them or had broken their home. But they never got mad at him. If they did, they never showed it. They also never showed any anger toward their step-father. He had been the only dad they had known for years, so they had a loyalty to him. And they didn't want to be mad at their mother. She was their mom. So when it came to taking out their anger about any kind of parenting, that left me. I was "safe." Gaining their respect, much less their trust, seemed impossible. I often wondered if I could go the distance. "Eighteen-minus-T and counting…"

My dad wrote a best-selling book in which he named a chapter "There's a Hole in the Door." I thought if I lived to write a book I'd name a chapter, "There Are Holes in *All* The Doors." By the time we moved out of our little house, only four doors remained unscathed—the doors from my bedroom to my bathroom and closet, and the pantry doors. The boys had thrown each other, or their hands or shoulders, into every other door in the house.

I clung to the belief that God had not set me up to fail but to suc-ceed. I believed that God had given me an assignment that only I could accomplish and that I could find a way to stand the pressure of adversity. I believed that the very Spirit of God filled me to help me achieve my God-given goals of seeing these kids turn into pro-ductive citizens and men of God. And as for those angels my friend called to tell me about after the disastrous counseling appointment, I was never big on angel theology, but I did call upon angels to guard and help my kids and keep them alive.

Sweet Relief

About a year after the boys came to live with us, we had some relief. Josh had been the main instigator of trouble during the first year, even though the psychologists had told us to keep an eye on Seth. They said at least Josh acted out his aggression, whereas Seth withheld his and was a simmering volcano, sure to erupt.

Josh's second school year with us was pretty much hassle-free. He bought a moped, got a job at the local grocery store and rode to work and back. He stopped stealing. His troubles at school became manageable. His grades rose. He still didn't study for tests, but he also didn't fail a single class. He started feeling good about himself.

Seth couldn't stand that much peace. He was still in that "scapegoat" role and served as a counterbalance to Josh's obedience by creating constant mayhem during the entire school year. Not a day passed without us entering some new drama or mopping up from the last one. Seth wasn't fighting as much as he did during his first year, but he was acting out in class.

That summer I had to go to see my parents in California for more than a week for business purposes. Richard knew that only one parent with two boys would spell disaster. As a reward for Josh's great year, I took him with me, and we had a wonderful time together. Josh, my mom and I went to Catalina by boat for a day, and Josh and I both got sick. Our time together was fun and funny, and after shopping, eating together and enjoying each other, Josh and I returned home with great memories.

The boys and I knew that being alone with Dad for more than a week was a reward for Seth as well. Seth and Richard both enjoy having time just to sit around, so they did videos, some projects around the house and very little housework. Richard's best friend, John, told Josh and me that at one point, it looked like every dish in the cabinets had been stacked on the counters. Richard and Seth did the dishes only once just before Josh and I returned.

By the end of that summer, Richard and I felt we had Seth "back" with us again. He was more respectful, obedient, and we had high hopes for the next school year. We talked about it, and everyone anticipated the start of school with great excitement.

The initial twenty-four months of blending were over. By all statistical accounts, we would now enter Cycle Two, a period of happiness that would last a couple of years until the children reached adolescence. But by this time Seth was fourteen and Josh was sixteen. Cycle Two lasted one summer. Or maybe one day. School started, and we cycled right on through to the next phase, with the boys erupting as they tried to separate themselves from us to fulfill their innate desire to become adult men.

Cycle Three

As if teenage boys are not enough of a handful, especially damaged teens, they also have their sexuality bursting from their pituitary glands. I discovered we didn't need to deal just with our own kids' sexuality, but with the sexuality of all the kids on the block, in the school, as well as in the church.

Boys attract girls. Saying girls are "forward" today is an understatement. The boys *expected* girls to call them. We had calls at all hours of the night. One young girl called in the middle of the night on a school night, and asked, "Is Josh there?" I opened an eye to look at the clock and felt my sleepy blood rising to my head.

"It is two o'clock in the morning," I said.

"So? Is Josh there?"

I hung up. Richard started a new rule, that if kids called after nine o'clock at night, the boys would be grounded for it. They were never grounded. The calls over which they'd claimed no control stopped, at least for a while.

Girls were everywhere. The boys seemed to feel they weren't alive if they didn't have a love interest. I'm sure it had to do with popularity and acceptance, but I also knew they had unresolved emotions with their mother, and a real problem in loving me. They didn't have a grown woman that didn't come with mixed emotions, so they looked for one their own age.

Richard and I talked with them about dating and relationships.

We didn't allow them to "go out," but we did allow them to see girls at activities we attended as a family. One time a girl who came over to see Seth a few times started liking Josh instead. That brought out all their codependent inability to be normal even with each other. Josh egged her on, even though he had another girlfriend, and paraded her affections in front of Seth as Seth simmered with anger. At one point Seth locked himself in his room. We intervened, but we could not change attitudes or emotions. The boys clung to their own world.

In stepfamilies, children are aware of their parents' sexuality more than in the nuclear family. Children don't think twice about a parent sleeping with another parent, but a parent who sleeps with a nonparent creates an awareness in the child that there's a reason for sleeping in the same bed.

Also in stepfamilies is the awareness of sexuality between stepsiblings. My cousin announced recently that she was marrying a man whose daughter is two years younger than her son. I suggested they set a good policy early, so it isn't awkward when the teen years roll around. She realized that modesty would have to prevail, and made a fun surprise out of buying matching robes for the entire family.

Stepfamilies also struggle with privacy, intrusions and setting limits. When a child crawls into the parents' bed and those parents have been married ten years, it can be charming. But when a child crawls into bed with newlyweds who have other things on their minds, it can feel like a major intrusion, especially for the stepparent in that bed. The parents' privacy has to be honored just as the child's does. Parents need some rules, but even more they need time away so they can let down their guard.

Our problem wasn't as much with kids crawling into our bed as with kids crawling out bedroom windows after dark to meet up with friends and girlfriends. Studies show that girls from divorced

No wonder...

homes experience sex earlier.[7] Four key indicators for early teens to engage in sex include living in a single-parent home, having no religious faith, living in a large city and doing poorly in school.[8] Girls without a father in the home are twice as likely to become teen moms.[9]

Sex is something every parent needs to talk about, and sooner than we think. My boys knew every reason not to have sex and every reason to keep their virginity, but stronger forces were at work. When the schools passed out condoms, that was permission enough. They could not say "no" when they didn't have a stronger "yes" built within them.

Richard and I continued to teach them how to stand on their own and the moral standard we believed in. This has proven to be a lifelong lesson, something they've had to work out on their own in order to believe as we do and live in a way that is consistent with their beliefs.

GET PAST THE PAST

Divorce affects a child's entire life and becomes that child's permanent identity. Because of that, a child deserves to know why that divorce happened. Unanswered questions have a way of becoming wild tales in the child's imagination, which could cause him or her to rebel. The "no fault" divorce is a legal term, not a moral one. Children left to themselves will always find fault. They don't understand how someone could think divorce would solve problems. For them, the divorce is the beginning of their problems.[10] The suffering a spouse endures in divorce is nothing to be compared with the suffering of the children.

When a child reaches the teen years, he might have to ask again what he asked when he was nine, because now he understands divorce on a new level. Children of divorce feel betrayed, like they've been lied to and convinced to believe in an illusion.

Parents can combat this by being honest. Facts give the child closure, tell the child the parent cares and demonstrate that the parent trusts him or her with the truth.

Several times Richard had to tell the boys the facts of the divorce—without embellishment, emotion or details. Richard admitted he hadn't been a good husband. He had been fresh from the drug culture when he married a church girl with a fantastic singing voice that should have made her a star in any church. But he didn't appreciate her or take care of the marriage. She made her mistakes as well. The boys idolized their dad so they hated hearing this, even though they liked being trusted with truth.

Parents who haven't worked through the emotions of their divorce might use such a time as a confessional, treating the children as one might treat a priest, trying to get the child to forgive them as a way to abolish their sins. This is too much emotional junk to heap on a little kid. Yet guilt does strange things even to grown-ups.

When it came to discipline, I sometimes wondered if Richard didn't let the boys get away with things he wouldn't have allowed had he not been dealing with unresolved guilt. Many struggles in stepfamilies stem from lingering guilt over choices parents have made. Parents struggle over the demise of the marriage, and sometimes the demise of someone else's as well.

The denomination Richard and I were part of would not ordain divorced persons who remarried. Other churches don't allow divorced persons to serve in leadership, and sometimes they are even prevented from singing in the choir. I had to work out the "second class" feeling I had from marrying a divorced man. It was hard to accept God's blessing on our blended family, even though some of the church's most famous leaders, such as C. S. Lewis, had married a divorcé. Kathryn Kuhlman both married and then divorced one. Did God strip them of their destiny because of

143

what they did? No way. I had to accept that my destiny was secure, and my job was to press into God and show those boys an open heart. But did guilt over Richard's divorce affect how I treated the boys, too? Did I "go easy" on them because I pitied them?

One day Richard was so angry about something, he lectured the boys. In the course of it, he became heated, raised his voice and burst out with: "And if you think I'm going to let you get away with this just because I feel guilty over the divorce, I'm not playing that game anymore. This is it. It's over. I don't feel one bit guilty. God has forgiven my guilt. You can't manipulate me with guilt because it is GONE!"

I have no idea if the boys had ever known their dad felt guilty or if their manipulations were anything more than a child's intuitive attempts to find a vulnerable part in a parent. But from that day on, something fundamental shifted in our home. It wasn't a specific behavior, nor did outward circumstances change, but it was as if a curse lifted off us. I knew that Richard had been praying over the boys in earnest, and I couldn't help but think that in answer to his prayer for them, God had met an even deeper need in Richard.

I think of King David fasting and praying while the baby he'd fathered out of wedlock lay at death's door. When the baby died, David got up to eat. The people around him were shocked, but David was living with life, not death. In a sense, Richard's getting over guilt was like getting over a death or a death sentence. He was choosing life.

Increasing Your Value

Our boys needed discipline in every sense of the word. Richard and I set out simple behavioral expectations. At first it was for them to brush their teeth, make their beds and do their homework. Richard also would say, "No sin in the house," which meant no immoral videos or music. In later years we added no smoking, sex or drugs on the premises and letting family members know where they were and when they could be expected home. We consulted books, professionals, educators, pastors and friends. Our rules remained the same, but we applied various consequences and motivations with the new ideas we gleaned. Experts agree that nothing works all the time for all the children.[11]

Each time we tried something new, life at our house would improve. Then the newness would wear off, and we'd try something else. We did things like the chart in the bedroom for daily activities. We attached rewards that might be immediate, weekly, big ones later or little ones now, financial rewards, privileges or all of the above. We contracted with the kids, getting their input to determine consequences for breaking the agreement. Consequences might be positive or negative or both. We taught goal-setting. We had them look things up in the dictionary and the Bible if they broke the rules or claimed ignorance. We gave every benefit of the doubt, yet we also tried to work through conflicts to help them develop.

As angry as I sometimes became, I adopted a slogan for myself: "If anger would make them change, they would have changed by now." My anger wasn't going to add one thing to my kids' lives except to motivate me. I had to find a better way.

Josh and Seth had three responses to discipline. One was that they blamed consequences on our "bad mood." They were convinced the world behaved in a random way, in which they were disciplined according to whim and rewarded the same. The more dysfunctional the family, the more random situations become. Cause and effect did not exist to the boys. They were subject to the caprice of adults who interfered in their lives, often in a negative way.

Another response was rebellion. Sometimes they took pride in being in trouble. They would push consequences to the limit to receive the worst consequence possible, as if proud that they could withstand the worst we could dole out. Richard and I partnered with the school. We told Seth he would be grounded at home if he was grounded at school. Seth accused us of "double punishment" and insisted his behavior at school had nothing to do with us. We weren't the rulers of the school. Why were we doing that to him?

A third response was obedience. But when they obeyed and received a reward, they didn't seem to understand how or why it happened. Regardless of how clear we were, positive reinforcement left them wondering what behavior was being reinforced. It was as if every moment stood alone, frozen in time, unconnected to the rest of life. An eternity was lived within a day, and the next day was its own entity, having no correlation to the previous day or the next day to come.

All the boys needed to do was string a few days together to see how great life could be after they stepped off the roller coaster of crummy behavior. It's like dieting. To lose weight, you need to string together a series of days during which you eat sensibly. Add enough days to that string, and you'll be trim. In discipline, all the boys needed was to string a series of days together during which they fulfilled daily goals, and they would have discovered that they could do the cool things they thought came randomly to lucky people.

Going back to the seven elements of a healthy child's life, we were stuck teaching our boys the first three again and again. We tried to develop their confidence in the fact that they had the ability to learn and grow. We let them know we loved, respected and needed them in the family. We taught them the influence they themselves had over their own fate. It was as if they were four- and five-year-olds in gigantic bodies, without any understanding that certain behaviors would bring predictable consequences. "Choices have consequences," we taught again and again. To change the consequences, change your choices. Until they understood that, they had no motivation for self-discipline, positive communication, responsibility or good decision-making.

Because we were "stuck" correcting and rechanneling the boys' energy, a counselor told us we had to raise our value as parents. In essence he said that as discipline increases, the value of the parent also must increase in the child's eye, so the child won't become even more rebellious. This is like Monty Roberts' horse-gentling—by bonding with the parent, the child will want to please the parent. Or like Dr. Dobson's advice that children need first to respect parents.

As a result, Richard and I raised the fun level and the interaction level in the house. We instituted "date nights" in which each of us took one of the boys out, then traded boys the next time. We did at least two date nights each month. Even if the boys were in trouble or grounded, date nights took priority. *Our attitudes became: Date yourself. Date your spouse. Date your kids.*

My dates with the boys were always quests for adventure, so it would at least be a fair consolation prize for not getting a night alone with Dad. Seth and I loved experimenting with various foods. Josh and I loved the IMAX theater and bowling and looking around downtown and cramming as much into a single evening as possible.

The boys loved these nights out. They just couldn't connect their behavior with the consequences. Josh often said we were "spoiling" them when we took them out. It wasn't spoiling. There were still the same rules. We were just having fun. They could not grasp that you could have fun and follow the rules at the same time. It amazed and frustrated me.

Once I was so frustrated with Seth, I didn't know what to do, so I took him to a restaurant. No agenda. I just took him there. I had been coming home from work early every day because Seth kept getting after-school detentions, often with Randy or Ryan, and I had to pick him up. But when I would get to the school, he'd be nowhere in sight. I knew the detentions were real because I'd checked with the school, yet he wasn't around. I would waste time that I could have spent working, or at least getting dinner started, while I sat waiting for him.

After about three days in a row like that, out of frustration, I found him and took him straight to a restaurant. I figured lecturing, scolding, letting him feel consequences wasn't working, so why kill myself? I'd raise the level of my value in his eyes instead. At the restaurant, I discovered I had little money, so I looked at the menu and suggested we split an appetizer of escargot. We received them buttery hot and garlicky-delicious. Seth had nothing to say for himself. I had nothing to say to him about his disappearances. We ate and made small talk. As he ate, he was seized with a sudden headache, and all we could figure was that he ate too much garlic. We went home.

In specific cases, bad behavior needs to be overlooked. If the child is just trying to get a rise out of us, then refusing to "reward" him or her with the expected reaction is the best way to get the behavior to stop. Psychologists call this "extinguishing" behavior. I don't know if that's what I did. I do know that we created a memory of the first time Seth tried snails and had to race home with a headache. I can't think of anything more that would have been accomplished by withholding overnight privileges with his friends on the weekend. I just had to love him enough to absorb his contempt and rebellion.

WICKED, WICKED, WICKED

"Oh yeah, you blend." That was the punch line of a garish hairdresser played by Marisa Tomei in the comedy film, *My Cousin Vinny,* when she and her New York boyfriend found themselves in a small Midwestern town. I remember seeing the movie on the weekend the boys ran away from home the first time. I laughed out of frustrated anxiety as much as anything.

Yeah, like you blend. As the only female in the house and the only one with a different DNA, I could have felt left out, but I found a few secrets to help me blend in, at least a little.

During times alone with the children, I discovered that members of families create something like an axis. Two family members will join together, become allies and leave other members out. Sometimes I was closer to Seth, sometimes to Josh, sometimes to Richard, and that's "normal." Josh and Seth's alliance often ended in disaster, so I would try to interject a parent to break that alliance and spare us.

In stepfamilies, at first the biological parent and child have a stronger alliance than the parent does with the new spouse. It's called the "insider-outsider" phenomenon. Breaking out of that "abnormal" pattern is important. Stepparents have to take it slow, but they do have to take steps! I discovered that by deliberate attempts to be part of each member's life, I was never left out. Depending on their receptivity, sometimes we just shared a joke or a favorite food or an activity. As a result, I felt a bond with them. As the axis changed, I never felt it was because I was "out."

Some stepparents hang back, thinking it's the biological parent's responsibility to thrust them into the "insider" group. *Every* parent must befriend children and stepchildren alike by finding common ground and spending time together. It's tempting to stick with our spouse and biological children, but sometimes we need to shake ourselves out of our comfort zones and take a risk to reach out to a child. If we don't shake ourselves now, we can be sure we'll be shaken later, by kids who feel no bond and aren't happy about our existence.

I also discovered in the revolving axis that the more I gave love, the more love there was. Love didn't run out, but instead expanded. When I was in alliance with Josh, I felt real love for him. Then the axis would shift, and my love would feel stronger for another member. If I drifted apart from a family member, which happened, I could always draw on those past feelings of love to get close to that member again. Because of that, I almost always felt someone in that home loved me, at least a little.

WEATHERING THE STORM

Regardless of what happened inside the home, I fought the wicked stepmother stereotype outside it. People assumed I was to blame for my sons' lack of discipline, that I was forcing my kids to be bad or that I was hurting them or imposing on them in some way. One time we had an altercation at the house serious enough for the police to come. I was shaken as I talked with them. Then I overheard the officers outside discussing the situation and saying, "Well, if she's just the stepmom and has moved into the boys' house…" I was grateful the police came, but in that low moment, I still had to explain I wasn't a bad person.

Another time we were required to report what our kids said to the Child Protective Services of another state. When we called, they yelled at *us*. Later in that state a child was killed while in court-ordered custody and outraged citizens made the government overhaul the CPS office.

People at church whom we didn't know thought Richard and I were nuts for loving and encouraging kids who had problems. Richard and I refused to add pressure by being embarrassed by the boys. And we tried not to embarrass our kids by pointing out bad behavior in front of people. For the most part, we corrected in private. As a result, people assumed either we caused or condoned poor behavior, were blind to the problems, were living in denial or were just stupid.

[handwritten margin note: Lisa always embarrasses Alisa in Public]

There Are Holes in All the Doors

All of this got under my skin on occasion. I remember one sleepless night sitting on the landing of our stairs, pouring out my heart to God. At one time I had driven cool, sporty cars, but I'd traded in my Firebird for a housewife mobile—a silver minivan. We had many good memories in that van, but it wasn't my kind of car. That night on the stairs, the van and everything else caved in on me. I said, "God, I don't have my own car anymore. I don't have my own house. I don't have my own checkbook. I don't even have my own bedroom!" A friend once said, "Maybe earth is just hell for some other planet." That's how I felt.

I would get angry with the boys when they did some crazy antic that upset their father. It seemed terribly unfair that I was the one who had to pay when he moved from a good mood to a bad mood, not because of anything I did, but because his sons delighted in causing trouble. Instead of having peaceful evenings at home together as we'd once had, each night we struggled with the "problem of the day."

Richard went through some job changes and unemployed periods of time during our first years with the boys. Unsteady work and chemical dependencies are two of the worst elements to affect stepfamily life. At least we didn't have chemical dependencies—not yet anyway. My work environment was in constant flux and was often stressful. As a result, I sometimes had no safe harbor at work, home or church. This left me feeling very mean and wicked!

Cutbacks came at work one time, and two of my best friends were laid off. That night the Gulf War broke out, and for the next two months I would come home and watch the war all evening while playing solitaire on my computer. At times I felt like I was paying all the bills to live in a house with crazy people. I wondered if I was the crazy one, paying for people to disrupt and destroy my life. The shock of what "family" would mean for

151

me came with slow, persistent intensity. I could not accept that I was going to raise kids who disobeyed and disrespected me, who had no loyalty to me or appreciation for me. In truth, this wasn't the situation. The reality was that my expectations for life were different from what I was getting, and I had to make adjustments.

I was committed, so I had to figure out how to keep my commitment and sanity without being robbed of justice and fairness. I found no books at that time to help me as a Christian parent in a blended family. We were "taboo," so it seemed we didn't exist. I was left with books that presumed I'd had these children since birth. I almost threw them across the Christian bookstore when I'd glance through and find the standard, "Start when they're young..." I never *had* young kids, but I still needed *help!* And I needed it *now!*

I also wanted to be a mother, and Richard was open to it, but that didn't happen for us. I wanted so much to feel a baby's tiny fingers, to see big-lashed eyes look up at me with trust, to receive notes from a first attempt at writing, to know when the child was angry there was still an abiding loyalty to me. Some of this was a natural maternal instinct. Some of it was escapism. It's easy for stepparents to escape to their illusions about their own children when the going gets tough. *A tough time isn't a good enough reason to make short shrift of stepchildren.*

If these boys were all I was going to get, if I had to get my children fully grown, then I still wanted to wrap them in my arms and tell them everything would be OK. If only I had it within my power to make everything OK. But there were few times afforded me to get that close. Instead, we just talked, and joked that the aspartame in Diet Coke would ruin their memories and solve their troubled childhood. Josh was more sensitive than Seth and would sometimes try to make me **feel** better by telling me he felt like I was his mother—something I knew he felt even stronger in reverse when he thought of her.

But regardless of any pain I went through, Josh and Seth had the worst of it. All children of divorce or death have the worst of it. It makes me cry today to think of how much my kids hurt back then. As our pastor at the time used to say, "Hurt people hurt people." Seth was a hurt and troubled little kid with man-sized cares crammed into a boy's body. He did not have the building blocks that "normal" kids grow up with—the understanding of cause and effect, the value of self-discipline, the belief that he could do something with his life, the underlying assurance that no matter what, his parents loved each other and him. Nor did he have the value system of a nation built by pioneers who believed that with hard work and perseverance, anything could be accomplished. Devoid of those basics, filled with rage, disturbed in his emotions—what hope was there for him ever to grow into normal manhood? I could not give up on him.

SETH— I grew up in a household with an angry stepfather. I won't even try to explain it, except I loved that man. He was the only dad I had from ages two to twelve. Even now, without a relationship with him, without seeing him more than once in the last several years, I still tend to justify his actions—not out of denial, but out of an understanding of his ignorance in what he did.

He was angry, and out of his anger came punishment that was random and excessive. I was never told about a set method of punishment for breaking given rules. Sometimes I would just get yelled at. Other times I would get hit or sent to my room. Sometimes I didn't get dinner. I didn't catch on to any real pattern. I didn't understand the meaning or the purpose of the punishment. It was unfair, and it made me angry. That's how I spent the ten most formative years of my life.

CAN STEPFAMILIES BE DONE RIGHT?

My brother and I felt alone in our childhood. There was my stepdad whom we often viewed as an enemy. There was my mother who was on the enemy's side. And there was my sister who had the blood relation to the enemy. Josh and I only had each other. To support each other and help each other cope with the hardship of an abusive home, we developed a psychologist's perfect model, a classic codependent relationship.

At twelve, I moved in with my father and stepmom, but my brother and I kept up the same relationship. My new parents tried to build a family. We fought it. They set up rules that we understood and agreed to. They explained to us the consequences of those rules. We agreed to those as well. Despite anything that was said or done, we lived as if there were no rules.

I don't know why, but fighting became a way of life for my brother and me. I have never been a morning person. When I wake up I don't spring out of bed and meet the day with joy. The phrase "bright-eyed and bushy-tailed" has never applied to me. I have since learned how to get the day rolling in a productive manner, but as a teenager, I didn't know how. I would wake up irritable, and my brother would immediately instigate. I barely had enough patience with him anyway, but in the mornings, patience didn't even have a chance to kick in before we started arguing over who was going to take a shower first, what to wear, who would go downstairs first. Whatever you could come up with, we viewed as competition and a reason to fight. We had no healthy way to cope, so we didn't cope—we just fought.

Fighting was just one of the destructive values I held as ideals. Productivity and accomplishment were never concrete to me. I relied instead on creativity and impulse. I didn't produce, but I created many things in my mind that I could produce if I wanted. I didn't accomplish, but I fulfilled my impulses, doing whatever came to mind. When I felt stress, I would get out of it in any way possible.

154

There Are Holes in All the Doors

Sometimes it was by fighting, sometimes by silence—which was basically repression—sometimes by hiding from or avoiding people, sometimes by confrontation, and mostly with good old anger. It took a lot of time as well as support from my parents to get to a point where I could replace my negative habits with constructive, positive habits that would allow me to produce and accomplish.

I remember my dad making a promise to my brother and me that he would never lay a hand on us. Not until recently did I realize his wisdom. In the beginning, I viewed my new parents' method of punishment as weak. I exercised blatant rebellion. It was annoying to get in trouble, but to me any consequences I faced were worth all the trouble of breaking the rules, as long as I got to have my own way.

Moving into a household with different rules, a different method of enforcement and different enforcers was confusing. Growing up with my mom, I obeyed most of the rules because they were what I was used to, the way things were done. When my dad did things differently, I would question and challenge new rules. I didn't have any respect for my dad's methods of discipline, and I didn't have any loyalty to my stepmom and father. At some point Josh and I realized we weren't obligated to our parents except through our respect for them. If we didn't have respect, then we didn't have to do what they asked, and we didn't have any obligation to pursue being part of their family.

It's amazing to me that I now feel the complete opposite. I have an immense respect for the rules to which my dad and stepmom held me accountable. I know that when I have children, much of my parenting will be done after the example that my dad and stepmom set. But this was a long time coming.

My stepfather had numerous affairs throughout his marriage to my mother. I don't remember any of those except one, but my brother says he always knew. Whether I knew consciously or not, I

155

still lived under an atmosphere of adultery and tolerance. My step-father had the affairs, and my mother tolerated them. I took on my mother's, rather than my stepfather's, attitude. I got involved in relationships in which I was taken advantage of, and I tolerated it.

I had a strong desire to be wanted. I always got a good feeling from knowing that a girl liked me. Even though my desire was strong to be accepted by women, I had a deep conviction about premarital sex. Unfortunately, because of the situations and friends that I exposed myself to, that conviction was buried. The character my parents exemplified and the principles they taught me helped bring that conviction into place again.

I was fifteen years old when I started to understand that I had issues to deal with from being the child of divorced parents. I had to get over the anger and hatred I had for my childhood. I had to come to terms with the injustice of my life, which I didn't want or ask for. Just as my dad had to deal with guilt, I had to deal with the guilt I felt for leaving my mom, sister and stepfather after growing up with them and sharing a life with them, no matter how dys-functional it was.

I think everyone who has been touched by divorce has been affected by it, so it is important to reconcile those issues. As a kid, you may think you weren't affected by the divorce, but that is unlikely. You have to get real honest in order to consider the impact divorce had on you, not because you might have a problem or two now, but to bring closure to anything that may cause future problems.

Back then I was in just a vicious cycle. A child who grows up in a dysfunctional home or is abused will, in most cases, create another dysfunctional home or abuse his own children. His chil-dren will, in turn, do the same with their children. I know the only reason I'm not in the groove of that vicious cycle is because my dad and stepmom broke it. I didn't appreciate it then, but now I know they not only saved me from years of unnecessary pain, but they also saved the children that I will someday have.

As much as I hated it, as hard as I rebelled, as much grief as I put them through, three things did it for me: God, love and consistency. My parents based every decision on God's principles. They loved my brother and me unconditionally and maintained a method of discipline that was clear and consistent. Every time I broke a rule they set up I received a fair consequence. I got angry. I rebelled. I cursed them. I ran away from home. I fought. Yet time and again they held me accountable. They never gave up.

In the household we were building together, my brother and I had one idea of family, and my parents had another. For one of those visions to be fulfilled, someone was going to have to change. It was my brother and I who changed. My parents never backed down. I threw every awful thing that I could at my stepmom to try and get things to go my way. It's like when you make a kid wash dishes, and he intentionally breaks a dish. Because you distrust him, you never make him wash dishes again. He got what he wanted, and as far as he's concerned he won. However, if he breaks that dish and then has to pay to replace it and still has to wash the dishes, it won't be long before he is washing the dishes without breaking them.

To this day, my parents require much of the same good behavior from me. I'm positive that if they had their own child, there wouldn't be any difference in their discipline, except the family would be minus some work they had to do to deal with our extreme dysfunction as young boys.

My parents' consistency of values was one of the biggest keys to my finally changing. Everything from those teen years is a blur of rebellion for which I felt justified. In hindsight, everything I did was horrible. My mind-set was totally in the wrong place. As my stepmom puts it, *boys don't think.*

My dad and stepmom increased their value to my brother and me, but not by doing what looked good in their own eyes. They did it by paying attention to what the issues were and figuring out what to do so that through our eyes we would see value in them. Once I had value in my parents, I could have value in their values.

For years, though, the more my parents helped, the less I wanted their help. I eventually got to the point that I left and wound up on my own. Only then did I begin to see that the values they had taught me were not for their amusement, but because they knew what would give me an enjoyable life. I began to understand that if I wanted to be happy, it didn't mean doing what I wanted. It meant putting things in motion that would fulfill God's destiny for my life.

My dad and stepmom's job was to share values with me that would help me obtain my destiny, my purpose for existing. And they needed to help me understand, in a practical way, the importance and benefit of those values. That's what took so long. Ironically, I learned to respect their values at a time of my life when they weren't even around to see it. Only when I was on the run or locked up in jail did I start to see what they had been talking about all those years.

My parents' consistency in their values was the key. "Train up a child in the way he should go, and when he is old he will not depart from it."[12] No matter how bad I was, that truth from the Bible was at work in my life, and no matter what I did, as my parents stood fast, this verse of Scripture was going to come true for me.

6

HE CALLED ME "IT"

JOANN— By the end of the boys' third year with us, we were pretty well in sync as a family. Conventional wisdom at the time said it took four to seven years for a stepfamily to start functioning as a family. With all we'd been through, I thought we were ahead.

The only serious problem was that Josh and Seth were still a mess at school. The previous year, Josh had struggled just to pass, and Seth and his friend Matt had created constant crisis. Seth's headmaster insinuated in our last parent meeting that either our child or Matt would have to leave. Since Matt lived closest to the school, we told the headmaster we'd take Seth elsewhere.

We told Seth that public school was out of the question. We knew he valued his old friends and popularity over his education, and we didn't want to invite that trouble. Seth decided on a private school nearby where he could pursue soccer. He would have to wear a uniform and cut his hair, but he agreed. At first.

Experts tell parents of teens to choose their fights, and looks didn't rank high on our list. With all we were dealing with, we didn't tell our boys how to choose their own clothes. We offered suggestions instead. We would say, "I think you may feel uncomfortable if you don't wear a button-down shirt." We were often not proud of how they looked, but we weren't going to allow our pride to affect our relationship with them.

Acceptance is more important than clothes. Clothes are a form of identity. To criticize teenagers' clothing can feel to them like you're criticizing them as individuals. As long as my children weren't in gang colors, or dressed immorally or disrespectfully, I was fine. All boys wore hats at the time, and since hats are at times disrespectful, I drew that line. They had to take their hats off at the dinner table, in church and for the flag and national anthem.

For a time, Seth wore men's size forty pants on his thirty-two-inch waist. I took him to dinner, church and Christian conferences any way he came, smiling and introducing him as if he were the best-dressed person in the room. At least he was alive, and he went…without a hat. After feeling embarrassed on occasion, he changed styles on his own.

With that said, it is also true that teens who look a certain way attract a certain crowd. Their looks affect their self-image, and their friends reinforce it. For more than a year, Seth had kept his hair long. It wasn't awful, but it was longer than most of his friends. It became his trademark as well as his idol. I have wondered if we should have made him cut his hair when he first started to grow it or if that would have just forced a crisis to come earlier.

THE FATALITY

For those first three years, I had continued to push the relationship with the boys' mother's side of the family. As the female in the house, it fell to me to keep the family's social plans rolling.

Everything came together that summer for the boys to go on visitation out of state to see her. They left, and a hush fell over our house. Richard and I slept for weeks and fell in love again. That's the summer my parents moved to Texas, so we went to California to help them move, and spent some time lying on the beach and relaxing.

We picked up the boys close to six weeks later, and they were altered. Not that their mother or stepfather had done anything to them. It was far the other way. The Other Parents had planned well for the visit and had taken the boys on a nice family vacation. But the boys were unable to handle the differences between the households or the emotional charge they felt. Seth's emerging emotions were new and raw.

Josh took his stepfather's last name that summer, as if in an effort to appease him. It was strange because Josh cared so much about being a "Webster man." But stronger forces prevailed. In that short time, they both fell back into habit patterns that had long since ceased, and they seemed more eager to act out once again. Their codependent behavior together intensified with Josh manipulating and Seth capitulating, then covering up. It was almost eerie to watch.

Days after their return to our house, Richard called to tell them to come home from a friend's house, but they refused. He told them again to come home, and they "ran away from home" in essence, defying their father and refusing to come back. I found them a few days later in the parking lot of a discount store. I told them they were ripping their dad apart and they needed to get in the van with me *right now*. Josh complied, then talked Seth into it. I didn't even care that I was using guilt as a club. I just wanted the episode over. I was angry.

During this time, Seth had been spending a great deal of time with a friend from church. The police called us at one point because the two of them had chalked the word "anarchy" on someone's driveway.

Within a few weeks, Seth bolted again. Since his return from his mom's he had been saying that he wouldn't go to the new school because he didn't want to cut his hair or wear a uniform. We reminded him that it had been his decision, and we were running out of schools. Soccer practice was starting in just a few days, before school began. We had what seemed like nonstop discussions about him attending. Richard and I hoped his love for soccer would push him over the edge to go. On the day of his first practice, Richard left work to pick him up, but Seth disappeared. We called the police, then started hearing through his friends about him showing up here and there. Reports came to us that he left because I wanted him to cut his hair. I was unreasonable. I was mean. He couldn't live with me.

After about two weeks, Seth started calling the house, sometimes twice a day, getting me or Josh or Richard. Josh tried to mediate. Richard tried to reason with him. I tried just to be patient, but I was mad. Once he called just to cuss me. Another time he told me he'd come back if we'd let him attend public school. I didn't want to be blackmailed. Another time he called to divorce us.

"Chris has this paper, and if you sign it, you won't have parental rights anymore."

"Seth, we *want* to be your parents."

"But if I get this paper, you won't have parental rights anymore."

"Seth, are you saying you're divorcing us?"

"No, just that you don't have to have parental rights."

"Seth, did you get a lawyer? Are you suing us? Why would we sign? You're our son. We *like* you being our son."

Click.

Richard met with him in person on these issues, apart from Josh or me, to negotiate and talk with him, but to no avail. Richard's best friend, John, tried to mediate, to bring some resolution to the impasse, but again to no avail. Richard was going to handle our family in one way. Seth wanted it another way. Richard wouldn't budge. Seth wouldn't either. It became a contest of wills, and they both knew Richard's was the stronger and that Richard was in the right. That seemed to make Seth madder.

One day, more than a month after he had left, Seth called Richard and said he was moving to his mother's house. He said he was leaving that night at midnight, and would come by to pick up his things at 7:00 P.M. Richard called me, stunned, yet feeling that at least we had a resolution. I had been angry because I was hurt. Now I was just hurt. I felt Seth was running away from facing the issues he was dealing with, issues that we'd tried to coax out of him for years.

Children who are allowed to move around between parents' houses end up falling outside the range of any true accountability. Parents lose track of who's in charge that week. The child changes all the rules, telling the Other Parents that's the way he does it at his house. He turns the tables. It becomes a quagmire of compromised parenting that doesn't work. We were entering dangerous territory.

I collected myself after Richard's call, then called all Seth's friends from church, all the schools, all our family and friends. I decided I wouldn't allow my son to sneak out of town but would at least give him a farewell and let him know we all cared about him and loved him. That night people crammed into our little house, upstairs and downstairs, and spilled out into the moonlit summer night.

The boys played football in the street, and everyone ate trays of food that friends brought over. Linda, who worked with me, brought Seth a giant plate of his favorite Reese's cookies, which no one can make like Linda. She gave him a card, and in it she had written Jeremiah 29:11: "For I know the thoughts that I think toward you, says the LORD, thoughts of peace and not of evil, to give you a future and a hope." Many other people wrote the same scripture in their cards for him. It didn't seem coincidental. That verse later became a promise for me about Seth's life.

At one point, Seth told Richard he needed a letter of permission signed so his mother would be able to seek medical care for him if needed, since she wasn't his legal guardian. Richard misunderstood him in the din of the crowd.

"You want me to sign it?" Richard said.

"One of you has to," Seth said. Then he added, "Yeah, you sign it. I don't want *It* to sign," and he flung his head toward me.

His friends crowded around him as if to protect him from me. It was surreal. And then he was gone.

PRAYER

Throughout the early years of stepfamily living, I had learned how to get real with God. I am not a morning person, but for the first time in my life, every morning I woke up early to make sure I had time to pray. When you know that the hour between 5:00 and 6:00 A.M. is the only time you'll have peace all day, there's something appealing about waking up.

Some people think they have to be holy for God, as if we can "fool" God into thinking we're something we're not. Or they think they need to "be strong" for God, when in fact He has promised to be strong for us. They want to tiptoe around and tell Him only what they think He wants to hear, so they don't hurt God's sensibilities or ruin their chances with Him.

The truth is, God knows who we are and where we are, and God cannot be shocked. He's watched the Khmer Rouge and Stalin and Hitler, and He's seen atrocities our history books don't even contain. He's heard the worst cussing, seen the worst attitudes, struggled with men whose sins are more outrageous than anything in our family. We can't shock Him. We don't have to fake it with God, or be "Super-Christian."

In the Bible, the great heroes of faith poured out their "complaints" to God. I took that tip and did the same. I learned that prayer was a safe place to express all my emotions, so I told God how unfair people were and what I thought about the life He'd given me. I told Him how hurt I was, how alone I felt, and what I thought He ought to be doing about it.

In prayer, I exhausted all the negative words I wanted to use on others. I sometimes even chewed out the boys or my husband when I was alone with God. I'd say, "If You were to allow me, this is what I'd tell them..." After I was finished, I would be amazed at how cruel I could be. I'd step back and say, "It's a good thing You didn't have me talk to them!" It was also a good thing I wasn't Jesus, or no one would have been forgiven. And it's a good thing I wasn't the Holy Spirit, or I'd have run out of this earth screaming. And it's a good thing I wasn't God, or everyone would be dead, including me!

Getting alone with God like that and telling the truth brought me close to Him. I felt so loved and appreciated when He didn't bonk me on the head for what I'd said or make me run out of gas that morning or something worse. After I exhausted my own feelings, then I would turn my attention to His feelings, to what He said about the situation. He loved my boys more than anyone on earth, and He had a wonderful plan for their lives that He wanted to accomplish. I chose to become His agent in their lives.

God didn't need anyone reminding Him of how awful the boys were. He knew more than I did. He needed someone who would stand in the gap between where they were and where He wanted to take them. My boys didn't need a judge—they needed an intercessor. Accusing them was just agreeing with Satan, "the accuser of the brethren." I needed to agree with God instead, and believe what He said about their lives.

I created a list of scriptures that I would pray over my family members and their extended family members. I would insert their names into verses like Ephesians 1:18, which asks that "the eyes of your understanding" be "enlightened." It was exciting to be like the apostle Paul who prayed for all his converts, who I'm sure drove him as crazy as my family sometimes drove me. I prayed Paul's prayers that he wrote to the churches over my own family.

I also learned that anger is a wonderful emotion when it is used as a motivator. I had never understood the verse, "Be angry, and do not sin."[1] I couldn't understand any purpose for anger except sin. Once I started getting honest with God, I used anger to drive me to prayer. I got so angry on a few nights, even after I'd prayed that morning, that I drove my car and parked somewhere safe. I couldn't wait to tell God how I felt. Then I'd use His Word to fight the battle in the spirit realm.

All the anger I felt toward my family either dissipated, or I used it against the devil. No way was Satan going to move in on the territory God had given to me. No way was Satan getting my kids and trashing our home. If Satan gets your stepchildren, you can believe he won't stop there. He's after *your* kids. It's not your spouse's kids who ruin your own. It's the devil that's ruining kids! You've made your decision. He's not after you anymore nearly as much as he's now after your children. I wanted to have the testimony of Jesus, who said, "Those whom You gave Me I have kept; and none of them is lost."[2]

In His Word, God often tells people, "Fear not!" I didn't want to fear my sons or our future. If God told me not to fear, then fear was within my power of choice. I rejected fear almost every day because I discovered it controlled me more than anything. I chose to live by faith, not by fear.

And I forgave and forgave and forgave. I didn't want to retain people's sins by unforgiveness. I didn't like people or their sin living in my head telling me what I would or wouldn't do, so I extricated them through forgiveness. I begged God in His mercy not to pay my kids back for their sins but to forgive them as well. I pleaded that we would not go through the difficulties in vain, but that He would bring a good result. I counted on God being slow to judgment but quick to blessing.

Regardless of what I said when I was mad, I didn't want anyone going to hell. Far from it. I wanted to see my vision for a happy family fulfilled, which included the boys' Other Parents. One of my favorite promises says this: "Surely there is an end; and thine expectation shall not be cut off."[3]

The more time I invested in prayer, the more I wanted to see a return on my investment. My dad says, "Prayer produces intimacy." Praying for the concerns of others gave me a vested interest in their lives, which knitted my heart together with theirs.

I prayed right out of the Bible that the walls of my house were called "Salvation," the gates were called "Praise," and the name of my house was, "The Lord Is There."[4] I prayed straight out of God's Word that no longer would violence be found within my gates, but that every place where I set my foot would be conquered for the kingdom of God, that salvation would come to both me and my household, that all my children would be taught of the Lord and great would be their peace and undisturbed composure.[5] A few times when the boys and Richard were away, I got wild, anointing my house with oil, praying over every room, taking authority over wickedness in high places, asking the Spirit of God to fill my house.

Then I would thank God. From a Bible teacher named Joy Dawson, I had learned as a young teenager to thank God in advance for what He was going to do. I thanked Him for hearing me, for answering my prayers and for doing what I couldn't see happening with my natural eyes.

Regardless of how horrible things became, I would move from expectation to sheer gratitude, finding things in the here-and-now for which I could thank Him. I thanked Him that the tree in the front yard was growing and the mailbox was standing. I thanked Him for every apple in the refrigerator and each stick of furniture in the house. I thanked Him that all I had to do was think and my hand would move, that I still had the two eyes, two legs and two hands I was born with. I thanked Him for cars that ran, for a dishwasher, a microwave, for everything we had with a motor.

I found friends who would pray with me sometimes. I remember my friend Camella, a stepmother, joined me on a few nights when we parked and prayed. It was fun to pray together. Much better than complaining to each other about something neither of us could change. I was invited to join a prayer group, and they became my closest allies. Samantha and Suzie and I prayed late into the night twice a month for five years. We *prayed!*

I often ended my prayers with, "As sure as I am that this floor is holding me up, that it won't crumble beneath me, that's how sure I am that You will do what You've promised me, that You won't let me go." I was sure He wouldn't let go of Seth either, even though Richard and I had to let go. For all that I had tried and for all that had failed, prayer was the single greatest thing I ever did for my family.

CHOOSE LIFE

Seth's departure brought a blessed calm to our home but a deep wound to my heart. Perhaps people around me seemed relieved he was gone because they didn't have to keep hearing about him, but I was crushed.

At first I cried for hours. My mind accused me that Seth left because he didn't want to live with *me.* He preferred his stepfather to *me*. Our relationship was the most intense failure I'd ever experienced. It was worse than my biggest heartbreak by a boyfriend. In Seth's case, I hadn't been "dating"—I had committed my mind, heart and soul to that child, and I felt he didn't want it. In that way it was like a divorce.

As the emotions subsided, I separated the feelings of rejection, hurt and anger so I could get to the reality of the situation. I knew Seth was just running, and he needed someone to forgive him and love him and pray for him as much or more than he always had. In one sense, nothing had changed. Richard had always told me I didn't need to knock myself out for the boys. I had no regrets for what I did, no regrets that I hadn't done enough. When I stopped doing, I just kept praying.

The stupidity I'd exercised in insisting on their contact with the other side of the family haunted me. My brother is older than I am, and he still can't remember my mother's birthday. Why did I put that burden and guilt on my boys? They just wanted to be where they were and not have to feel guilty about the Other Parents. Years would come later when they would have the emotional maturity to deal with it. And their mother was already dealing with it as an adult.

Richard never blamed or condemned me. Having come from a dysfunctional home, he realized more than anyone the years the boys had ahead of them in which they would continue working out their problems. He and I had a commitment to each other, to the marriage and to the boys, a commitment that stood strong. As long as our marriage didn't disintegrate, our stepfamily still had a chance to survive.

The second time I received what seemed like a "call from God" came during the boys' second year with us. I had stayed home from work, something I almost never did. But I was exhausted by the boys and needed time alone. I remember that I ended up doing laundry that day, and was folding clothes in the living room when the telephone rang. My friend Mary Jean Pidgeon was on the other end. She was the mother in a yours-mine-and-ours step-family where she and her husband each brought a child from another marriage plus had one of their own. I poured out my heart to her.

Mary Jean said, "Remember, Joann, light will always swallow up darkness, love will always swallow up hatred, and life will always swallow up death." We prayed, and I thanked her before hanging up the telephone. Then I sat on my living room floor and cried.

"God," I said, "I'm in over my head, and all You can do is have someone recite some poetry to me!"

About a month later as I struggled with something new, a vague memory came back to me. I called Mary Jean and asked her what she'd said.

Light will always swallow up darkness.

Love will always swallow up hatred.

Life will always swallow up death.

I'd known Jesus as the Way and the Truth, but not really as the Life that He is. I'd never understood that God was love and light and life and that nothing could be stronger than those. At one time, that would have sounded silly to me, too ethereal, meant for people who floated instead of walked. But I learned that by choosing love, light and life, I was choosing God's side, which swallowed up hatred, darkness and death. God has set before us life and death, blessing and cursing, and *commanded* us to choose life. I could choose to bless or to curse, to have life or death. I chose blessing, not cursing. I chose life, not death. In a relationship with a difficult family, choosing life meant to choose what produced life, not concen-trating on negative behaviors and attitudes that brought darkness, gloom or a figurative "death." Love, light and life repel evil. *I deter-mined in my heart that my love would outlast their hatred.*

My relationship with Seth was dead when he left. Josh would call to check up on him, since Josh was the only person in our home to whom Seth wanted to speak. Richard, Josh and I wrote on occasion and sent Christmas gifts, but we heard back only once. Seth wrote to us six months after leaving, addressing us as "Webster," without the "dear" or even "Mr. and Mrs." In the letter was a demand for money for his birthday rather than a gift.

This was an opportunity to choose life. Seth wanted to create death. He wanted to be filled with hatred. We knew he wouldn't even understand his own letter for twenty or thirty years, when he had his own teenager. We didn't demand an apology, nor give in to his demands. Richard and I ignored the letter, except Richard interpreted correctly that Seth wanted money because he was starting into drugs. But we did send a gift.

The Bible says that when we forgive our enemies and pray for them, we heap burning coals upon their heads.[6] We heaped coals on Seth. The kinder we were, the madder he got. But that wasn't our problem. We were going to do right. He'd have to choose his own response.

THE PATTERN

I have a friend who is estranged from his son right now. The last time the son came on visitation, the boy provoked a physical altercation, then called the police. The police came, and even though the child recanted, the officers said an arrest had to be made. They took the dad to jail. The dad is a high school coach, a profession in which he can ill afford being charged with child abuse. He is preparing to stand trial right now and struggling with how to handle his son. The boy has relented and promised not to press charges, so the hope is that the matter will drop. Yet being extricated from legal problems doesn't solve the bigger problem. What does he do with that child?

171

CAN STEPFAMILIES BE DONE RIGHT?

Stepfamilies don't generally escalate into violence or experience this degree of difficulty, yet some do. Stepfamilies don't generally deal with abused or diseased children, yet some do. God's principles apply across the board, to every family, nuclear or blended, and when followed, they bring positive results.

1. Forgive.

Forgiveness doesn't mean the other person was right or that you have to accept him or her in the same way and on the same terms. Forgiveness doesn't mean nothing happened. Forgiveness means you acknowledge the evil, but regardless of what happened, you won't let that sin lodge in your heart. God said if we forgive others, He'll forgive us.

2. Don't quit.

If we quit we fail. God never gives up on you. Don't you give up on God. God has a plan for your family, your spouse and your kids. If He can just get one person in the situation—you—doing the right thing, then He has a foot in the door to bring the rest of the family around. Every breath you take says God hasn't given up on you, His child, so don't you give up on your child.

3. Pray.

The late revivalist Leonard Ravenhill said, "God doesn't answer prayer. He answers desperate prayer." Emotions of anger, fear and depression can help us press further into God. Make Him, not the neighbor or your best friend, your primary confidant.

4. Accept.

We have to accept who our children are and come to terms with what our children do with their lives. Just as we are "accepted in the Beloved" because of Christ's unconditional love, our spouses, children and stepchildren need us to stand in Christ's stead on their behalf and accept them even when we disagree.

5. Be prepared.

The best way to prepare is to read the Bible every day, even if only a few paragraphs. You don't know what will happen tonight or tomorrow morning. Every situation will be shaped by the Word that is in the forefront of your mind. My dad says not to pray for opportunities, but to pray that we'll be prepared when opportunities come. Opportunities for good or for evil surround us every day. We are the ones who determine their outcome.

6. Look for the truth in the situation.

With Seth's horrid letter, Richard or I could have taken that opportunity to say: "That's it! This child is never setting foot in this house again!" But we saw in that letter a hurt little kid who wanted to be remembered with a birthday present from his parents, so we sent one. Finding the truth is like picking out a melody playing on someone's car radio when you're in a loud, smelly traffic jam. Finding the truth gives you a key to adjust your attitude to get through.

7. Keep communicating.

That means listening even more than talking.

My coach friend is struggling to discern the truth with his son. Does he let the child know he's forgiven him? Would the child interpret forgiveness as a license to do the same again? Can he allow that child back in the house, knowing that physical violence may be the result?

We could fill hundreds of pages with scenarios of stepfamilies, and your family would still be different. But if we act on principle, the answers will always be similar. God managed to write a finite book of roughly fifteen hundred pages that includes everything we need to know about life or the future. Even though your life is unique compared with billions of other people alive and dead, those principles and patterns for living will still solve and resolve every situation you are in.

CAN STEPFAMILIES BE DONE RIGHT?

Seth left, but I had no idea we were not even halfway through our "tale of woe." Yet good, terrific, positive things were happening within both of us. We just didn't know yet what they were. Sticking to the principles, rather than living by personality or preferences, made the difference.

THEY'RE *BAAAACK*

Seth left, so it was up to Josh to destroy the peace. He continued to fail in school, and his previous year's upstanding citizenship disintegrated. Yet we all kept trying. Josh took the missions trip alone that Thanksgiving to the orphanage in Mexico where he and Seth had gone together the previous year. Josh was finding who he was apart from Seth. He continued to refine his tastes and even wanted to attend the musical "Annie Get Your Gun" for his eighteenth birthday celebration. That was the same birthday when Richard brought home what looked like a cute tabby kitten, which turned into our finicky family cat, Tiger. Even after Richard taught Tiger to box, Josh never claimed him.

That summer, Richard and I started talking with Seth again and invited him to come on summer visitation and go on a family holiday with us. We were going to drive across country to see Richard's family in the northwest, then down to Northern California to help my sister move to Texas to join the rest of my family. I knew it was going to be a long, wonderful road trip with plenty of memories we'd never forget.

Josh and I went to the Dallas bus station and picked up someone who called himself Seth. He'd grown several inches, shaved his head and his face had become that of an adult. He looked angry, hard and afraid. Richard got off work that night, and we all celebrated Seth's homecoming as a family. In just three days, we'd be back in the good ole silver minivan, buzzing across the country like previous summer vacations.

Richard gave Seth a few simple rules. No drugs, no sex, no smoking. He told Seth no overnight stays with friends before we left because we were all needed to get ready. The next day, Richard and the boys ran errands, and Seth called a few of his friends, one of whom was an eighteen-year-old with a car. That night, we did something fun involving me and the boys singing a crazy song to Richard and having a cake. As soon as we finished, Seth's friend drove up, and Seth said, "Gotta go." Richard said, "You're leaving?" Seth jetted out the door. I asked Richard what he was going to do if Seth didn't come back that night.

"I don't know."

Richard looked defeated. Seth didn't return, and we didn't know what to do. We couldn't leave Seth because he was in our custody. If anything were to happen, he was our responsibility. Richard decided to call the police. An officer called the young man's house, and the young man defied the officer.

"I'm eighteen. I can take responsibility for him."

"If you're eighteen," the officer said, "then when I get to your house, if Seth's not there, you're going to be arrested for kidnapping."

The officer went to the young man's house and brought Seth to ours. Seth started in on Richard, saying he was sorry and that he'd never do it again. Richard told him to wait downstairs while he prayed. I can't imagine what Richard went through alone with God. It is one of the worst things a parent ever has to do. But he had to do it. He called me at work to ask if he were making the right decision, and I tried to console him. He called the airlines and spent a chunk of our vacation money on a same-day ticket to send Seth back to his mother. We couldn't even trust Seth on a bus, because he could cash in the ticket at the first stop and turn back.

Three sober Websters started the next day on our big adventure without our Seth. Each day of the trip, Richard seemed to heal and grow stronger, realizing what a disaster such a trip would have been with a rebellious child who flaunted his disobedience.

That was all we saw of Seth for eighteen months, just those two days during that one summer.

A year after Seth moved away, Josh got fed up with school and with us. He felt we were too confining, too strict. He had not accepted that we wanted to have input into his life to help him. The defining moment came when we refused once again to allow him to spend the night at a girlfriend's house. I remember after receiving his angry phone call that night, I turned to Richard and said, "I can't take it anymore." I've often wondered if God heard and acted on my behalf. It had been four years, and I was tired.

Josh left in October. For Thanksgiving, my entire family went to Orlando, Florida, with all the nieces and nephews, and it was wonderful, even though we missed our boys. Richard and I had a pleasant, quiet Christmas and sent them gifts. Then, in January, I received a call from one of the boys' friends, Rick.

"Mrs. Webster, I thought you should know that Josh and Seth are back in town."

My mind had just started to relax, and the numbness of what had gone on in our home was just wearing off. My prayer life had become a time of joy instead of agony, and I felt "normal" again. It seemed like all that calm and peace drained out of me for a few moments before I collected myself and told myself once again that God had set us up for success, not for failure.

I called Richard to tell him, then I turned to my computer and changed my screensaver to read, "Jesus Loves Joann." I figured I needed all the encouragement I could get. We later heard the boys had been caught with drugs at their high school and had left town rather than waiting to be expelled. Days passed, and we heard about them showing up here and there.

Then one day I was driving home from work in my MGB roadster, which I'd had since college and kept stored in the garage. A car full of young men pulled up beside me on the freeway and started waving to me. I thought they were strangers admiring the car, then I figured they were the boys' friends, so I pulled over. The young men tumbled out of the car, and I saw my own sons dressed like druggie-hoodlums. I hugged them. And I asked if they intended to call their dad, and they promised they would.

That was when the revolving door started in our home. At first, the boys dealt drugs from a friend's house and were happy in their crime. Then they regretted dropping out of school, so they asked to move in with us and start school. They came with a friend. Then one left, the other stayed. That one left, the other came back. At first Richard wouldn't allow them upstairs. They had to earn their way up from the ground floor, literally. Sometimes they didn't like the rules and left on their own. Sometimes we had to ask them to leave if they broke the rules. Neither of them finished high school.

"Toughlove" was popular in the eighties, resulting from parents who needed help to control their teens. Those involved didn't want to send their children out on the streets, so they developed local chapters where parents could band together and if necessary, send their teens to another parents' house for a time. Some of my stepfamily friends did this with their children. If nothing else, it gives parents and children alike time to blow off steam and get some emotional distance before trying again.

"Toughlove" advocates that parents cannot be manipulated by their children if they:

· Set limits and stick to them.

· Keep in touch with schools, counselors and a network of support.

· Stop needing to trust their children.

177

- Check out how they respond to their children with others who know them.

- Accept and recognize how their children manipulate them.

- Rid themselves of false parental pride.

- Have self-acceptance rather than self-hate.[7]

These are last-ditch efforts, but at least "Toughlove" parents don't quit. Richard and I set our rules and let the children fend for themselves. We provided the prayer protection, and as the years would prove, angels did show up. The Bible says angels are sent out to care for God's people.[8] We learned of drunk-driving accidents and others dying, but our children were spared, and we knew God was proving Himself strong on their behalf.

Richard and I banked on the fact that if the boys were hungry or in trouble, they knew we loved them and that we would help them. We'd worked for years to set the standard before them, and for years to give them every opportunity to respect us and respect our standard. We trusted God that His principles would work. Otherwise we had nothing.

SETH— Tiger our cat is the worst pet I have ever known or even heard about. I moved home after running away and then living with my mom, and the cat was just *there*. All I wanted was to be with my parents again, but the cat came with the deal.

At first I was excited that we had a new pet. I reached out to him and tried to build a bond, but the cat wasn't having it. Tiger was apparently distraught over me moving into his home and invading his space. He was loyal to my parents and only exhibited two emotions that I could tell, one was love for my parents and the second was a hatred for me.

Tiger would hiss when I walked into a room. If I left the door to my room cracked open, he would take the opportunity to make his way in, sniff around for something important and then relieve himself all over it. Many times I climbed into bed exhausted, slipped my feet into the cool sheets ready to snuggle under my comforter and put my tired body to rest, only to find that the sheets weren't cool, but wet.

This became an ongoing battle. The cat was out to get me even though I tried over and over again to get him to like me. He took advantage of my leaving my door ajar. He disrespected me. Hated me. It was hopeless. That cat had alienated me in every attempt to have a relationship with him. Nothing worked.

Sound familiar? Through Tiger, I learned a little of what it was like to be in my stepmother's place—to move into a new life, eager to develop relationships, only to find that the harder you tried the more you were hated. I could try to psychoanalyze my reasons for treating my stepmom the way I did. I might call it misdirected hatred and resentment, inability to develop a relationship out of a fear of betrayal, inner turmoil. But I wasn't thinking about any of this as a kid. None of it crossed my mind. She was there. I was there. I didn't want her where I was.

For a while, though, I had a pretty good stretch of emotional stability. My dad, stepmom, and my brother and I had a healthy relationship going as I recall it. I was still getting into trouble at school, but I was putting more emphasis into learning. I became involved in basketball, band, drama and enjoyed science and other subjects. The only problem I can remember was the influence that I allowed my friends to have on me. I was stealing with them, getting into fights, picking up girls. I even lost my virginity while hanging out with them. Even though things were going pretty well at home I had all the same issues. I had just found what I thought was a better way to work the system than in direct rebellion to it.

In my mind, I had resolved that after I went to private school for a year and did decently then my parents would trust me enough to send me back to public school. It didn't work out that way. They said I was going to have to go back to private school, and the one I had to go to was the same one that my brother was going to. I would have to cut my hair and wear a uniform. I agreed to this in a fleeting moment of sanity. Then I got a whole other idea.

I went on normal summer visitation, this time to my mom's. My stepdad had joined the military and was stationed closer to Texas than where they'd been on the West Coast. Going on visitation at age fifteen, I had a repeat experience from when I was twelve, only in reverse. This time it was my mom and stepdad who were fun. We spent a week at a lake resort during that visitation and just had an all-around good time. I wanted to dye my hair black, and Mom did it for me. My mother also empathized with my desire to go to public school. Once again I thought I'd found that ideal household I was looking for. During that visit I resolved not to go to private school or cut my hair. Basically, I didn't want to do what my dad and stepmom wanted me to do.

Back in Texas, I came at my parents full force. I pushed the issue that I didn't want to cut my hair. I insisted that I was going back to public school. I had decided the direction of my life, and I was ready to force my parents to conform to my desire. They didn't. I couldn't win, so I left. I moved in with a couple of friends and their single mom, having convinced her that my parents were unreasonable. I couldn't stay there long-term so I stayed with a couple of other friends off and on. The summer ended and school started up, but I couldn't get enrolled in school, and no one's parents would let me stay with them. All my friends were back in classes having fun, but I was alone. One friend helped. He would have me drop him off at work and then I would take his car to the lake and just sleep. I had isolated myself, but even in that condition, I felt that I had freedom from rules and ideas I didn't agree with, so I was a noble martyr.

The joy of this lifestyle soon wore thin, so still feeling I'd won a victory, I called my mother. I explained to her the unfair treatment I had received and asked her if I could move back with her. That's when I called my dad to say I would come by and pick up my things. I just wanted to go, pick up my stuff and leave. No attachments, no commitments. I got to the house and everyone I knew was there. I was excited to be the center of attention, excited to flaunt my newfound freedom, but I also felt like my stepmom was trying to make me feel bad. I thought she was trying to make sure all our friends knew that she was a good guy and I was a bad guy—that I was choosing to leave, not that she was running me out. I hated her for having everyone there. I hated that she wouldn't leave me alone. I just hated. I decided ahead of time I wasn't going to say a word to her that night, and I thought I was being considerate in referring to her as "It," rather than what I really wanted to say.

This isn't one of my proudest moments, but I'm glad that through my stepmom's attitude, extreme situations like this didn't kill our relationship. We both became stronger because of it. It was going to take a lot more than I thought back then to earn freedom.

Going to live with my biological mom was in some ways good for me. For one, just after I left, the kids in my dad's quiet little suburb got into heroin. Some died. Maybe my move kept me from getting killed.

It was also good to get away from my codependence with my brother. Making friends on my own gave me confidence. When my brother left my dad's and came to live with me and my mom, a lot of my friends didn't even like him. I felt bad for him, but I felt good that I had my own identity. The distance and time broke a lot of the need I had for my brother's acceptance.

When I returned on summer visitation, I didn't expect my dad and stepmom to enforce their rules, even though they had told me they would. I thought that because I didn't live there, I should be able to make my own decisions. When my dad said not to spend the night with anyone, I decided that was my opportunity to show them I was in charge of my own life and would live it as I pleased. I was shocked and embarrassed to be sent back to my mom's after only three days. But they had my attention now.

Dropping out of school to return to Texas was a good move for me, as strange as that may sound, and for all the wrong reasons. I had become involved in drugs of all kinds and adopted the lifestyle of raves and parties and the drug deals that went with them. Right after I returned to my dad's, a friend was at a pay phone hooking up some drugs for our friends when he was shot and killed. I was usually the one to mastermind those deals, so if I had still been there, I know I would have been the one in the phone booth.

After returning home from Missouri I found that, in a way, I was maturing a little. As I went in and out of my dad and stepmom's home, things seemed to move smoother. I had more of an acceptance for the rules and a good understanding of what consequences would come by choosing not to follow them. My parents made it clear that they weren't going to tolerate my breaking the rules, but that they would do everything in their power to be a support for me.

As I matured, I began to feel more and more distraught in the lifestyle I was stuck in, but I wasn't really trying to find a way out. My life was heading on a downward spiral and even with my parent's support, I knew that I was going to need to make some kind of a change, or it was all going to cave in on me.

7

SURVIVE
AND THRIVE

JOANN— In a landmark, twenty-five-year study, Dr. Judith Wallerstein has found that the negative effects of divorce increase in children throughout their teen years and into adulthood. Children of divorce enter adolescence early and have a prolonged adolescence. They are "late bloomers" who often don't complete college. In her study, 40 percent didn't marry. As she interviewed ninety-three children who grew up through divorce and forty-four counterparts who did not, Dr. Wallerstein recorded that children with unhappy parents who stayed together ended up better off than children with unhappy parents who divorced.[1]

Dr. Wallerstein's study is not very popular among divorce attorneys and some of her colleagues who insist that children can become emotionally and psychologically balanced even after divorce. Divorce attorneys today are the "experts" parents turn to when asking about divorce. That's kind of like a plump kid going to

CAN STEPFAMILIES BE DONE RIGHT?

Hansel and Gretel's witch to ask for help dieting. Dr. Wallerstein has the numbers divorce attorneys don't want to hear, even though every member of every stepfamily knows from experience that the children suffer. The old "they'll adjust" line used by parents to justify divorce is only that—a line. It cannot be substantiated or defended. The average stepchild's confusion, anger, displacement and flight from betrayal is well-documented.

I discovered by experience what Dr. Wallerstein reported, that my children's and their friends' adolescence was prolonged. We can't write them off at age eighteen or twenty-one. We can't give up on kids. The Bible says, "Save some by snatching them as from the very flames of hell itself. And as for others, help them to find the Lord by being kind to them . . ."² Children are our "inheritance." Our door was open as long as they lived by the rules. It was inconvenient to be quiet for people sleeping on the living room couch, and our house constricted so much from extra bodies that Richard and I sometimes treated the local Starbucks as a living room. But my kids and their friends needed a little extra help. My idea of counting backward from eighteen evaporated. It was a bad idea anyway.

Richard and I grew stronger during these later years. Instead of figuring into the 60 percent of stepfamily parents who divorce, we went beyond surviving. We thrived. Commitment is the number one key to successful stepfamilies. By joining together to face our problems, Richard and I drew closer in purpose and became less affected by differences. We discovered, as Richard puts it, that being married isn't a matter of finding the "right" person, but adjusting to the "real" person.

We also developed a philosophy that God is not concerned just about our happiness, but also about our holiness. Often during the '90s I heard people talking about their "rights" and how they "deserved" something. But the Bible says it's God who gave us rights, and apart from Christ we deserve hell. That's why we need Jesus. I don't advocate a martyr attitude that makes us suffer in order to be holy. Christ already suffered everything for us. But it's also not right to close our hearts to people just because opening our heart hurts or is inconvenient.

Many times during those years I would ask myself, "What would Mother Teresa do?" This was before Mother Teresa died and before "What Would Jesus Do?" became a popular slogan. I asked it because Mother Teresa seemed to be the very image of calm assurance. No matter what came her way, she was able to rise above it and administer the love of God. But 99 percent of the time when I asked myself that question, I determined that Mother Teresa would not have noticed there *was* a problem. She didn't see people yelling or cursing at her. She saw people who needed Jesus.

Mother Teresa's life didn't revolve around her. She was busy doing what Jesus said: "I was hungry and you gave Me food: I was thirsty and you gave Me drink. . . . Inasmuch as you did it to one of the least of these My brethren, you did it to Me."[3] That's what I wanted to learn. Instead of taking insults personally, I longed to be able to see the hurting person behind the insult. Instead of feeling the squeeze of too many people or not enough money, I longed to be able to see God the Provider take care of me as I took care of those He sent my way.

I'm not suggesting I made a dent toward becoming Mother Teresa! *I needed more love.* God wants us to love "strangers and foreigners," but how can we love them if we can't love the children He's put in our own homes? We *can* learn to fill our homes with love! Love is the strongest thing on earth because love *never* fails and love covers a *multitude* of sins. Regardless of how much we strained under the constraints of a small house, under the pressure of the boys having to fit a new standard and accept values foreign to them, under the stress of parents and teachers and church people looking at me and Richard like we were idiots for raising hellions, under the constraints of finances and the tension of unmet expectations— regardless of it all, love would *never* fail.

What Else Could Go Wrong?

The trip Richard, Josh and I took without Seth that one summer became a comedy of errors. We picked up my sister to move her to Texas, but we couldn't fit all her possessions in the truck we rented. We changed vehicles, unloaded and loaded. Later we lost keys, lost each other and the trucks overheated. At one point, I was looking at the map as my sister drove one of the vehicles. Lois was insistent we'd make good time now because, "What else could possibly go wrong?!" Almost two hours later, we discovered we were on the wrong freeway going in the wrong direction and were hundreds of miles away from the rest of the family. For a week we could hardly look at each other without bursting out laughing.

Just when you think nothing else could go wrong, something just might. And yet, by the time it does, it doesn't have to hurt. We can even laugh.

In the revolving door days at the Websters I learned, adapted, came more into my own as a person, trusted God more and felt less worried about what would happen to the boys. As a family, Richard and I vacationed with whomever was home, cooked together, laughed together and had those fabulous long talks into the wee hours of the morning.

We had to ask kids to leave from time to time. The biggest problems came if we left town without them. It was infrequent, but we had to take precautions. That's what "Toughlove" says about not feeling like we have to trust our children. We do better if we're realistic. One time one of the boys had a drug deal planned at our house. Another time they'd arranged to have a party. Another time they succeeded in having a party. One time I had to have the locks changed because someone, unnamed, wouldn't give me his key. I lost my temper that time, but other than that, Richard and I held to the standard in a calm manner, asked the boys to leave if they didn't abide by the rules, and we welcomed them back if they wanted to try again.

It wasn't hard to see my kids' guilt. I could tell in their crummy attitudes if they were doing wrong. I was happy that at least they felt guilt, at least they were figuring out right from wrong. Once we had charges for 900 calls on our phone bill for pornography. We changed services so that dialing long distance from our home would require a code. One time our cable television company bill had $100 in charges from pay-per-view films, mostly pornographic. At first the company refused to do anything about it, so I went to a city council meeting and explained that any boy could rent those movies in his house without his parent's permission or knowledge. The case I presented made front-page news in the Metro section of the *Fort Worth Star Telegram* and the cable company changed their policy. The company also reimbursed us for the charges. We adjusted our house rules to include "no pornography."

Both boys ended up in jail from time to time for not taking care of traffic tickets that became warrants for arrest. We allowed them to work it out themselves, allowing them to learn that they were capable people who didn't need Mom and Dad to bail them out. It was a hard line, and we were criticized by friends, but it worked.

At one point, Josh had warrants in several neighboring communities. One city picked him up, and the police department relayed that information to the other cities. When Josh finished serving time in one city jail, they sent him to another and then to another to serve out his time for each warrant. Josh called with a desperate voice many times, but we didn't bail him out. Family members and friends called to ask what they should say when Josh called. We told them we hoped they would love him, but love him enough not to bail him out.

Josh is a doer. He is never bored. In each city, he ended up working to help the police. He reorganized the officer's filing system or cleaned or helped answer phones for them. Seth, on the other hand, would sit and sulk and fight. In one jail cell an inmate called him "girlfriend" one too many times, and the man discovered how fortunate he was that officers were nearby to protect him.

Over the years, the boys responded in their own way to what they saw at home. Both started seeing a pattern, a cause-and-effect consequence attached to their behavior. They saw the values that Richard and I took years to merge, and they saw our resolve, which became a comfort to them. Regardless of how crazy life got "out there," they always knew where their parents were and where they stood in their parents' eyes. It is amazing to me that for bright boys, catching on took so long!

Then we discovered what else could possibly go wrong. Seth was arrested, but not just for a traffic ticket. It was a felony arrest for a large amount of LSD.

THE SENTENCE

Just over a year after the boys returned to the area, living with us off and on, they went to the store one evening, and Seth ended up in jail. Josh bailed him out, and that's when Seth left for Mexico, only to call months later saying he'd try to live by the rules if he could move in until his court date.

On the morning of his trial, we picked up Josh where he was living and prayed on the way to court. Seth was adamant about throwing himself on the mercy of the court. He said he had prayed and that he wanted to trust God to let him off the hook as far as jail time. I didn't know if it was one more manipulation, or if he had heard from God, but I was ready to give him the benefit of the doubt one more time. I never dreamed I'd have to offer that benefit of the doubt before a judge.

But there I was on the witness stand, trying not to fiddle with my pearls, being questioned by Seth's attorney, then the prosecutor and now the judge, who was trying to figure out how Seth came out of our family and yet ended up in so much trouble.

"We're just a regular law-abiding family," I told the judge. "My sister was a prosecutor in California for thirteen years. My brother-in-law was a deputy sheriff right here. My father has an international ministry, and I work for him. We're just normal people who are doing the best we can with these kids. Seth is going to turn out OK in time, but he doesn't need this felony hanging over his head for the rest of his life."

After a few final questions from the judge, I was dismissed to step down. I expected Seth's lawyer to ask Richard to take the stand, but no one else was called. Just me. Once again, I felt like a stepmom on trial. Would I forgive and defend this child? Of course. Richard squeezed my hand as I edged past Josh's long legs and slid onto the bench next to him. The judge waited a few moments to look at something on his desk, then he looked up and addressed Seth.

"Son, according to your mama, you're a real smart boy, but you've been doing some real stupid stuff. I want to ask you a few things." He asked about how Seth started doing drugs when he lived out of state and just wanted to be cool. Then he asked about the job Seth had landed with his girlfriend's dad, and Seth's plans. "What would keep you from showing up in this courtroom again if I let you go free today?"

Richard and I almost stopped breathing. Seth looked so young and skinny from the back with the enormous judge's bench beyond him and the powerful man staring down as if he could see right through him. Seth hesitated before he answered.

"This right here," Seth croaked out, losing his voice. I'd seen his red-rimmed eyes, but I hadn't realized he was crying. It was only the third time in ten years that I'd seen him cry.

"What?" the judge said.

"This right here. What I'm going through today is enough to keep me from wanting to come back," Seth said.

I released my breath and my grip on Richard's hand. What a great answer. Seth didn't try to hype the judge, didn't beg for mercy, didn't tell him some Boy Scout story of all he was going to do when he got off. He told the truth. Like the school principal years earlier who had admired the way Seth accepted discipline for that hallway brawl, this judge, it seemed to me, was impressed.

The judge shuffled some papers and gave the sentence. Deferred adjudication. Seth would have to spend two years on probation, pay court and probation costs and do hours upon hours of community service. But no jail time if he stayed clean.

"You said you live at home right now?" the judge asked.

"Yes, sir."

"Well, I think that's the best place for you. I want to see you stay there." He hesitated, then gave us our sentence. "No, I'm *ordering* you to stay there until your probation ends."

Richard and I sat frozen to the bench.

"And don't ever show up in my courtroom again because if I see your face, I'll lock you up!"

That was it.

Seth received his sentence, and we received ours. Two more years! We all hugged and Richard treated everyone to a lunch celebration. I was worried about Seth's attitude, but still felt happy he would be with us because I enjoyed him. Seth seemed ambivalent, happy to be free but not expecting to be stuck with us! I'm sure he thought he'd be on his way out the door now that he had accomplished his goal of living with us to look good to the judge. Instead he was going to have to live by rules he had violated for years.

Growing Up

Seth stayed at our house after that, but Josh was in and out, leaving for four whole years to live in California before he returned. Upon his return, I discovered that some traits were inextricable parts of their "nations." Some were good, like Josh's cooking and care in his dress. Some were bad. One of those was Seth's forgetfulness. No matter what we had done with Seth in his childhood—teaching, disciplining, scolding, warning, fining him, creating lists—he had always been forgetful.

One year we had bought a brand-new coat for Seth to wear during Christmas vacation when we visited Richard's family in the Northwest. Seth begged and nagged until we let him wear his coat to school for the first time on the last day before Christmas. Sure enough, he took it off and left it. We raced to the school late that afternoon, arriving minutes after the last janitor left, and found a notice on the doors, "Any coats left over Christmas vacation will be given to charity."

Later when I saw Seth as his own man, I realized how futile it had been to try to change him. The older a child is when the family "blends," the less the parents are able to change those ingrained habits. We frustrate ourselves and the child and break the peace of our homes by struggling over things that only the child can change. The coat was a big deal at the time, but other things weren't. If Seth wanted to change his forgetfulness, Seth was going to have to do it himself.

Who would have thought that with his freedom riding on it, Seth would lose the paper documenting most of his community service hours? His parole officer gave him a week to bring in a new paper, or he would be in violation of his probation and he'd be going to jail. He worked night and day to finish almost all the hours again that had taken over a month, plus keep up his regular job. This was a terrific lesson for him.

Seth struggled with our house rules as he tried to figure out how to stay in the house without being kicked out. He spent most weekends at his friend Randy's apartment. We had a rule about letting us know where you are, and also about attending church at least once weekly. He struggled with those. His attitude was good, so we would just remind him and let it slide. Once again I took a back seat to Richard's discipline. Often I felt Seth stepped over the line, but Richard would meet with him and allow him to stay.

As hard as it is to quit smoking, drugs or drinking, it is far harder to change self-image, worth and value. Over time, Seth changed. A new attitude I'd never seen in him began to form—appreciation. He knew we did for him what we didn't need to do. Now when other kids who stayed with us broke the rules, he was outraged on our behalf. He grew sensible, loyal, grateful.

A few years after he moved in for good, Seth and I were talking about the "bad ole days" in one of our long conversations. He asked, "Did I ever apologize for that?"

"No."

"I'm sorry," he said. He meant it. My kids had learned, as most children do, to make forced apologies: "Go tell your brother you're sorry." "I'm sorry." Those apologies serve as good life lessons but don't always mean anything on the part of the child. The day Seth knew *why* he should apologize, and was willing to apologize, was a tremendous triumph.

GETTING OVER IT

The experts say that stepfamily parents must:

- Imbue values

- Affirm boundaries
- Provide a structure
- Establish rules for moral and productive living
- Affirm the children[4]

Fulfilling this list was a years-long process for us, not something we could take care of in one family council or one late-night conversation. Family counseling had helped Richard and me more than the boys, because it guided us in what to do. In a way, not having the resources to continue extensive counseling may have been a blessing because we had to learn to take care of our problems within the family. We had to learn and grow ourselves, which was good.

Later, Richard went over the "Making Peace With Your Past" workbook with our sons. It is designed for people from dysfunctional families, but it is a tremendous tool for growth, regardless of a person's background. I went through it as well.

Strange things helped the boys as they matured through their prolonged, probably divorce-induced adolescence. Right after the ill-fated summer experience with Seth, Richard and I had found a stray Border collie mutt that looked like a dog I'd once owned named Jodi. We brought this dog home, and she turned out to be the smartest, best dog we've ever had. Jodi B, as we named her, served in some respect as a catalyst for the family during the revolving-door period. She was something we all owned equally and no one owned exclusively. None of us was more related to her than another. She loved each of us and was always excited to see any of us come through the door.

From what I've read, this isn't just "dog therapy." Often when people have another child, either biologically or by adoption, that child brings the family together. An adopted child doesn't have anyone's genes, so everyone is equally related. The biological child carries some of the same genes as every member of the family. The new child likes the attention of each family member. The only thing that can ruin the yours-mine-and-ours stepfamily is if one of the parents becomes possessive with his or her child. If a biological mother doesn't want her new child around the step-children, that will alienate the family, when in fact the opportunity exists to help unite the family. All we had to offer was a stray dog, but she did a great job.

Seth pressed on. He left the warehouse job, then went to work at a gas station. Kids copy what they see more than what they hear, and Seth's work ethic now came out. He aroused my admiration one morning that winter when the roads iced over, and he was one of the few people who showed up for work, just like his dad, driving the beat-up Honda he'd bought with his money from his first job.

A customer at the gas station was so impressed with Seth, he offered him a job at a new restaurant that was opening. Seth took it and did well, exercising customer service and practicing Spanish with his coworkers. His ears were pierced, and he still wore his pierced earrings, and he had a tattoo by that time. He was living a bit loose, but he was still light-years ahead of where he'd been. Because Seth had a steady job, a friend sold him a Jeep, which was the biggest thing that had happened to him.

Then one afternoon, I looked up when I felt someone's presence in my office, and Seth was standing there. He was unshaved and shaking like he gets when he's nervous or excited.

"I need to change jobs," he said.

"What happened?"

"I can't make it with God if I stay with those people at that job. I'm going to be just like them."

I didn't know what to say. We were doing a lot of work at the time, and I could have used another pair of hands, at least for a while, but we didn't have full-time work available.

"I can give you some hours, but I don't know what you need."

"If you could give me twenty hours a week, I can find a second job, but I have to get out."

I looked at him, trying to understand where this was coming from. I made a decision to test him.

"Seth, if you're going to do it, then I want you to start work tomorrow, so you have to go there and give them two weeks notice right now. After you give your notice today, you can work out your schedule to work both jobs for two weeks, and we'll take it from there."

We prayed, and he cried, then he left and resigned from that job that day.

CHANGED!

Seth grew like a weed drunk on Miracle Grow when he changed work environments. He made new friends, and everything in his life, from my perspective, changed at once. He broke up with his long-term girlfriend and decided not to date anymore. He worked hard, and worked hard at getting along with others. It was as if everything we'd ever taught him was boiled down into a few months and all of a sudden he got it.

I remember one day he made a deposit at the bank, and they credited it to his savings account instead of his checking account. Checks bounced, and he owed hundreds of dollars in bank fees. Several times I urged him to go to the bank to talk to them, but he wouldn't. As I was on my way there one day, I asked if he'd ride along. He agreed. He told a customer service person what happened, and she pulled out a form to reverse all the charges. He seemed a foot taller when he walked out. It wasn't about the bank. He learned how to face a problem head-on without fear and without trying to manipulate the outcome.

We were still friends with Franklin, who had come to dinner when Seth was a young teen and made an impact on Seth's life by admiring his artwork. Franklin came to work with us, and became Seth's supervisor. Seth learned computers, graphic arts, Web site design and marketing, and made his career choice. His understanding deepened, which drove up his confidence and self-esteem. Today he's working full time in Internet technology and going to school full time.

What is great about watching Seth change is to realize how much I changed, too. I have a saying taped to my computer, "We are never more like God than when we give." I know thousands of stepfamily parents struggle with wanting their problems to go away so they can have the life they expect or desire. But we can have it in spite of the struggles, if we are willing to give ourselves to others. If we'll strengthen our marriages and raise our children to the best of our abilities, we can trust God to take care of us. His Word says it is His "good pleasure" to give us the kingdom. He doesn't begrudge us a good life.

Seth has joked that he made me the person I am today. He is absolutely right, no question, in the same way the movie about the *Titanic* disaster made Leonardo DiCaprio a star. I had an opportunity for the biggest tragedy of my life, including divorce or worse, but I opened my heart to God, and He turned it around for the better. An idealistic child who watched presidents and leaders assassinated, whose friends came home from war hooked on heroin, I had become cynical before I was old enough to know the definition. At a young age I had discovered the world was often a horrible place, and I could have stayed in my cynicism forever. Instead, the first three years of stepfamily life challenged and changed me in ways even a college education and thirty years in church never did.

Sometimes I could feel the change coming. I would remark to myself, "I'm growing more mature right this instant." I'll never forget when I gained self-confidence. My friend Milan remarked to me during the first year we had the boys that I seemed like a self-confident person. I laughed at him and said that underneath I was a scaredy-cat. A few years later at another dinner party, I saw him and remembered his statement. By that time I couldn't remember the scaredy-cat me. Self-esteem developed. I became more understanding and responsible. I grew calmer and happier, while becoming less angry, worried, insecure, self-conscious and inferior-feeling.

I started stepfamily life without a clue that I was stepping outside my comfort zone. Through it, I learned how to get along with diffi-cult people. I learned how to listen and display genuine concern. I found out that if I never preached a sermon in my life, I could still make an impact on just *one person*—and that counted. I became a person who could receive from others. I developed deep friend-ships. Controversy and conflict in relationships stopped frightening me. My prayer life became vibrant and alive. I received more of God's love than I'd ever known, and my heart enlarged to be able to love Him back. As all that was happening, I rose to become CEO of my dad's ministry, and then at the age I'd targeted years earlier, I quit my job and started writing full time, which was my dream. The old me could never have taken this course. Only the person my step-family helped me become could do this.

Some people try to learn everything but don't get around to applying anything they've learned. It's better to learn just one thing and apply it than to know hundreds of things we don't apply. Richard could have gone on Prozac, I could have gone on Valium, Josh on Ritalin and Seth on lithium. We could have coasted on a family "high" until the turbulence stopped. I could have retreated into depression or denial. Instead, I dealt with each day as it came and tried to apply each lesson I learned, not knowing that by doing so, I was going to become more of the person I'd always wanted to be. I will never get over being in a stepfamily, and I never want to. My family is the best thing that ever happened to me.

SETH— Life isn't a sitcom where all our problems are resolved in thirty minutes. Being bad seemed fun to me for a long time. I was comfortable with it. I could make others laugh with it. No consequence I suffered after leaving my first home was concrete. The Alternate Education Program at school was the first "jail" I was in. I would be bad, and they'd put me in the AEP room all day long. But such consequences were inconveniences that were temporary and tolerable.

I viewed authority as a temporary obstruction that kept me from doing what I wanted to do. But I was going to do what I wanted, no matter what. Authority only stalled me. I never looked at someone in authority and thought, *Wait a minute, I should listen to this person because they might know something.* Instead I regarded them as a nuisance and never gave them a second thought. Even when I was arrested for drugs, I argued with the officer because I had no respect for him and thought I could talk my way out of it.

The only concrete things in adult life are death and jail. At first it was scary, but jail even lost its intimidation after the first couple times. I would stay one or two nights, then I'd be out. Yet even I started noticing that the older I got, each time I had to suffer a consequence, it was more severe. I finally realized it was going to keep getting worse. What scared me was when I became afraid of what I'd become. I'd never allowed anyone to know the real Seth, and now I'd lost sight of him, too. After my felony arrest, the consequences weren't just temporary. They came from a perpetual thing, a cause-and-effect thing that I hadn't understood. Facing a real penitentiary was scary.

It was only in jail that my dad's discipline made sense to me, and after five days I realized what a child I'd been. I always pushed until something concrete stopped me, and this was it. I felt like a fool, but thanks to Dad I knew what to do, at least in part.

I would love to tell you that everything in my life became perfect after that, but it hasn't. Solving problems, like those caused by divorce and blended families, can take a lifetime to work through. At the writing of this book I am twenty-three, and my life is just beginning. I'm now able to apply the principles that I should have learned and been exercising when I was eighteen. Instead, at eighteen I was in a court case on trial for a felony drug-possession arrest.

I sat there looking at my stepmother take the stand with poise and confidence. She looked like she had done this a hundred times. What was going on didn't seem to faze her. I even wondered at one moment if she realized what kind of trouble I was in. As the minutes passed by and they asked her more questions, I grew more afraid. I liked what she was saying and didn't want my mom to come off that stand. I didn't want the judge to make a decision. Out of the corner of my eye I thought I saw the bailiff getting a pair of handcuffs ready for me. I was terrified of what I had become and the consequence I now was facing.

My stepmom stepped off the witness stand and made her way back to the audience with my father, brother and girlfriend. I took a brief look back at them, thinking it was the last time I was going to see them, at least while wearing civilian clothes. The judge called my name and my attention was brought back to the situation. He asked me some questions, then asked what would keep me from returning to his courtroom.

I looked him right in the eyes and with a tear streaming down my face I said, "Your Honor, this right here."

I thank God that He put mercy in the heart of that judge. In a few moments, the man considered what he heard, weighed the truth and saw the sincerity in both my stepmom and me. He made a gracious decision to let me go with the minimum—two years' probation with a hundred hours of community service.

There you have it. My rock bottom. That should have been a life-changing experience. Once again, it wasn't. The truth was that

I wasn't any better walking outdoors with my family afterward than I was when I walked into that courtroom. I still had the same problems. I just had a chance to deal with them in society instead of in a cage.

Events can be life-changing, and yet we all have to keep living after that defining moment, and that means making the right decision each and every day. We all expect a burning bush to appear, or that giant to fall dead from a slingshot wound, and then our *Something amazing to happen* lives will be perfect, we think. It doesn't work that way. Moses denied the responsibility of the burning bush outright until God gave him help to speak to the pharaoh. After killing Goliath, David committed adultery and then murdered the woman's husband to cover the sin. We have to keep working at becoming who God has for us to become. It takes time.

After the court case, I went through ups and downs. I made mistakes. I did end up back in that judge's courtroom, and I received an inexplicable second reprieve. I had problems to deal with, like manipulative relationships, destructive friendships and a love for evil—which is a whole other book. But a progression took place in my life, and one by one those problems fell away.

The first thing I did was choose not to quit. I came to a realization late in my life, by most standards, that my actions had consequences. Though the consequences for my decisions seemed overwhelming, I stuck it out. With God's grace and my parents' support I made it through the tough parts. I wanted to give up. Running away to Mexico tells you that much. But I knew in my heart, because of what my parents taught me, that God had more for my life, and I didn't have to settle for less.

The second thing was learning to change my desires. Just because I was sick of the results I was getting didn't mean that I had a desire to do right. It was the consequences of the bad decisions that I didn't like. I still liked the bad things themselves. I had to choose to do right by gritty self-discipline, only because I knew I didn't want the consequences of what I was doing wrong. I did right because I had to, not because I wanted to. As time went on, I started reaping benefits for right decisions. That was a surprise. I never knew how great it felt. That's when I began to desire to do right. Now I get more satisfaction from making right choices than I do by indulging in the wrong.

The third thing I had to do was to cut off unhealthy relationships. Josh and I grew up with a manipulative and codependent relationship. I had lived my life justifying that relationship. As sick as it was, I thought it was normal. I didn't realize my need for codependency until I broke up with the girlfriend I dated for four years. As I sought God, He made it clear that my problem wasn't the girlfriend or the relationship—it was my need for codependency and for a partner in relationship who was manipulative. I had never had such a crystal-clear revelation of how I worked as a person.

It blew my mind that when I started to change and seek God's plan for my life, He was willing to heal me on all levels, including socially, with relationships. I learned that bad company corrupts good character. For me to be able to continue, it just came to me that I had to cut off the friendships that hindered my growth. When you've determined to do right, the people around you can ruin everything. You cannot see the benefit of doing right when everyone around you is doing wrong. Rewards aren't immediate. You need to separate yourself so you don't become blind to them altogether. Cutting off bad relationships allows you to see clearly the incomparable life of living right.

The fourth major step was my spiritual growth. I can attribute any areas of growth in my life to this one thing. I knew through all the years from age twelve to twenty-one that I needed something. I had a hunger for something deep. I had a desire for a relationship with God that I never knew how to fulfill. Once I made a decision

201

to do right, and cut off my friendships, I trusted God to put me where He wanted me and to do what He wanted to do with my life.

The fifth and final step in my progression came because God saw my sincerity in wanting Him to do what He wanted to do with my life. Yet He tested me, so that I could realize and see my own sincerity. I had been working for my grandfather, at the time, for two years. I went to work for him on a whim because I didn't want to be with some friends from my previous job who had corruptive natures. I knew I could get a job with the family, so I made a decision to do what I knew to be the right thing.

Once there, I started tithing and giving more than I ever had in my life. I still had outstanding traffic tickets and warrants that would crop up, and with Jeep payments and insurance, I was broke most of the time. But I paid tithes even when it hurt, and God came through for me with surprises in my finances. The job was great, learning graphic design and Web design. I found something that I loved and wanted to do.

Then came cutbacks, and my job was axed. I couldn't believe it at first. I had to ask myself what I was going to do. Would I go back to damaging others in order to vent my emotions? Instead, I trusted that God had full control of my life. He came through again, giving me a better job making twice as much. I am now in management and have received almost a 100 percent pay increase since I started. I learned that applying God's principles for finances to my life brings increase. I tithe on every dollar and pray for where to spend the rest. I give offerings at the church at just about every opportunity and have received blessing upon blessing from the Lord.

Because of my dysfunctional background, it took me years to learn the fundamentals of God's truth for my life. I had to get through all that junk to get back to the beginning. My parent's perseverance led me into a life of repentance, reconciliation, responsibility and relationships. It takes time, but God will do it for you, too.

God's Blessing on Stepfamilies

JOANN— People shouldn't think twice about getting a divorce. They should think fifty thousand times, or fifty million times, and then they still shouldn't do it. You never know who your ex-spouse is going to bring into your children's lives. The odds are stacked against you and them for any future happiness. And yet, God is merciful and compassionate and kind. If the task of blending a family were impossible, God would never have put Joseph in that position with Jesus. God would never have allowed divorce even for a minute, nor would He have put up with polygamy even one time, if there were no way to succeed afterward. As Dr. Wallerstein writes, "Yes, it can be done. Yes, it's much harder than you think."[5] I told myself a thousand times, and I'll tell you now, God doesn't set you up to fail. He sets you up to succeed.

Marriage is sacred to God. Second marriages are sacred as well, or we could divorce the first time with impunity and then add a string of marriages like notches in a belt because they wouldn't matter. Second marriages matter. God says whatever happened to get you into this situation, repent and go on with life, sinning no more. When we repent and choose life, He promises to give us a *more abundant* life. Watching the horror of divorce eat away at our children can cause us to relive the pain, step back or descend into condemnation. But we can press into God to keep our spirits healthy, to make our new marriages vibrant and to step in and become a healing agent in our children's and stepchildren's lives.

God has not raised His hand of judgment against stepfamilies. God blesses blended families. He knows we need His help. He is more than willing to give it. The past is over. Every opportunity that comes you can use for the good. God will show you the way.

EPILOGUE

THE WAY WE ARE

JOANN— Our family changed in startling ways while Seth and I wrote this book. He proposed to, and then married, a young woman whom he had known for years, Shamain. Seth defied the odds for children of divorce by taking the most important step in marriage, which is the first step—setting a standard and choosing a spouse.

Most children of divorce fear making commitments and the vulnerability of intimacy. They feel lost and unprepared to make a life choice, or unworthy of choosing. Many have trouble dealing with normal conflict, for fear of it escalating, and some find that their anxiety and fear increases when they should feel most content.

Seth overcame a victim mentality by praying about previous relationships. That started the end of his codependent behavior. Shamain is also a child of divorce, and together they are sifting through the dregs left in their minds and hearts that could keep them from achieving their vision for a family. Many children of divorce repeat the mistakes of their parents, even though they are intent on giving their children a better childhood than they experienced. Seth and Shamain are actively fighting this, with their future based on a deep, shared faith.

As Seth and Shamain worked through their expectations and communication styles during their engagement, my only challenge was to help plan a wedding with all the various families involved. Miss Manners became my best friend. I felt for Seth's mom. She was halfway across the country, and the first of her children was getting married. So I called her, and she appreciated my concern. We talked several times, and her openness amazed me.

Seth's mom came three days before the wedding, joined by just her daughter because she had long since divorced Seth's stepdad. The night she arrived, I saw her for the first time since the day in the courtroom when I'd received custody of her children. It could have been awkward, but she had come with an open heart and was eager to help make her son's day special. She was easy to be around with such a terrific attitude. We spent most of the three days thrown together as we did our parts to make the wedding happen.

We enjoyed each other. On the day of the wedding, we went to the hairdresser together, and after the reception ended and her family was gone, she and her daughter came to our house for the post-wedding celebration. We sat side by side in my dining room eating snacks and laughing about the funny things that had happened during the course of the last three days. She also sang a song at the table, just to be funny, but I got to hear that beautiful voice the boys had always bragged about. When they left long after midnight, Seth's sister said, "Oh no, we have to leave, just when we've bonded!" It was a scene just like in my dreams from a decade before. A wonderful, satisfying, rich, heartfelt miracle. The proverbial "icing on the cake."

CAN STEPFAMILIES BE DONE RIGHT?

Josh moved out during the same week Seth married. About a week later, he passed his high school equivalency exam on the first try, after fearing and avoiding it for six years. We had cake, gave him a gift and joked that a GED was our family's idea of graduation. Now he has high hopes of entering chef's school and pursuing his dreams in earnest. Josh is still working out issues from the past on one hand, and on the other is almost too fun-loving for his own good. My hope for him is that he settles down and becomes serious about his career but that he will cry when he laughs and will laugh every day.

Richard and I live in an empty house with just the dog and cat, Jodi B. and Tiger. I unpacked my china and crystal, which I've never used, since I no longer fear for its life. Richard and I love our solitude, our life together, and have our dreams and plans for the future intact. We often have Saturday morning breakfasts with Josh, Seth, Shamain and sometimes their friends or cousins. It's delightful to see them come, delightful to see them go.

Recently I was praying, telling God how much I love my life now and how grateful I am for where I am. No price seems too great to have such peace and fulfillment, and to stand before God knowing I've done my best. I said, "God, I would pay any price to have this life." I felt as if God answered by saying to my heart, "I would pay any price for you to have it."

That's exactly what He did, sacrificing His own happiness, His Son's life, so I could have a life that is more than anything I dreamed possible. He's done that for everyone equally. He's done that for you when you accept His Son.

Seth wanted to end this book with letters to each other to help bring closure to a season that has passed. We trust that seeing what God did in our lives will touch yours, and that some of the richness of our experience will leave a deposit in your life as well.

JOANN—

Dear Seth,

You have enriched my life and caused me to stretch, think, grow, pray and become more of the person God wanted me to be all along. I know God put me in your life for my love to help save you from yourself. I know He put you in my life so He could save me from myself. We both win.

It is exciting for me to watch you. You're now an adult without a child inside screaming to come out. You're being the real you, not pretending, not having to be strong, not struggling after an elusive image. You are a man of substance and courage. I admire you for it.

I said earlier in the book that the child often disguises the seed of greatness, and you used some despicable disguises. But the mask has been removed, and the "you" God planned from the creation of the universe and knit together in your mother's womb is emerging. You have only begun to discover the talents, abilities, strengths and creativity God has placed within you. I know as you continue to press into Him, God will uncover more than you ever thought could be contained within one person.

Grandpa says, "God puts no limits on faith, and faith puts no limits on God." To that I would add, God puts no limits on you if you'll put no limits on God. I believe in you, love you and can hardly wait to see everything you accomplish.

If helping to raise you was the worst thing that ever happened to me, then life is good and the world is a wonderful place to live—because raising you was also the best thing I ever did. Thank you for being part of my life and for letting me be part of yours.

SETH— Dear Mom,

In the time I've grown from childhood into manhood, I've learned to appreciate the sacrifices you made for me. I came into your home and your life in my greatest time of need. You gave me love, support and an example that was crucial to my development in becoming the man I am today.

I know God ordained our relationship and, as is His way, has done what is best for us both. I am glad to know that we have overcome.

Your perseverance and adherence to God's destiny for our lives has birthed a relationship as strong and intimate as if we were of the same blood. In the spirit realm, it is the same blood, the blood of Christ.

Grandpa says, "Love desires to benefit another, even at the expense of self." You are the reality of that truth in my life.

I love you and thank you.

NOTES

CHAPTER 1
WHAT IS YOUR VISION?

1. Proverbs 23:7
2. Jeremiah 29:11
3. Dr. James Bray and John Kelly, *Stepfamilies: Love, Marriage, and Parenting in the First Decade* (New York: Broadway Books, 1998), 11.
4. Jane Nelson, *Positive Discipline* (New York: Ballantine Books, 1987).
5. Ibid.
6. Ibid.

CHAPTER 2
MERGING VALUES

1. Bray and Kelly, *Stepfamilies,* 106.
2. Ibid., 16.

CHAPTER 3
BUILDING UNITY

1. Delores Curran, *Traits of a Healthy Family* (HarperSan Francisco, 1983), 31.
2. Tom Hopkins, *How to Master the Art of Selling* (New York: Warner Books, 1994).
3. Hebrews 11:3
4. Bray and Kelly, *Stepfamilies,* 42.
5. Ibid., 41.
6. John 20:23

CHAPTER 4
PEOPLE NEED PEOPLE

1. Nelson, *Positive Discipline,* 47.
2. Stephen H. Glenn, Ph.D., and Jane Nelson, Ed. D., *Raising Self-Reliant Children in a Self-Indulgent World* (Roseville, CA: Prima Publishing, 2000).
3. Ibid., 34.

4.   Psalm 101:6, TLB

5.   Glenn and Nelson, *Raising Self-Reliant Children . . .*, 17.

6.   Bray and Kelly, *Stepfamilies*, 214.

7.   Ephesians 6:12

8.   Mark 4:39

9.   Mark 14:61

10. Ephesians 6:13

11. Matthew 6:21

12. Tommy Barnett, *There's a Miracle in Your House* (Lake Mary, FL: Creation House, 1993), 55.

13. Judith Wallerstein, *The Unexpected Legacy of Divorce* (New York: Hyperion, 2000), 74.

14. 1 Corinthians 15:33, NIV

CHAPTER 5
THERE ARE HOLES IN ALL THE DOORS

1.   Nelson, *Positive Discipline*, 135.

2.   Glenn and Nelson, *Raising Self-Reliant Children . . .*, 48.

3.   Ibid., 49–50.

4.   Dr. James C. Dobson, *Dare to Discipline* (Wheaton, IL: Tyndale, 1987).

5.   Bray and Kelly, *Stepfamilies*, 16.

6.   Proverbs 29:1

7.   Wallerstein, *The Unexpected Legacy of Divorce*, 188, 299.

8.   Pat Centrer, "Broken Home Key Factor in Early Teen Sex," September 21, 2000, Christianity.com, citing pediatric researchers from the School of Medicine at the University of Minnesota.

9.   Ibid.

10. Wallerstein, *The Unexpected Legacy of Divorce*, 92–93.

11. Nelson, *Positive Discipline*, 135.

12. Proverbs 22:6

CHAPTER 6
HE CALLED ME "IT"

1.   Ephesians 4:26

2.   John 17:12

3.   Proverbs 23:18, KJV

4.   See Isaiah 60:18; Ezekiel 48:35.

5.   See Isaiah 60:18; Acts 16:31; Joshua 1:3; Isaiah 54:13.

6.   Proverbs 25:22

7.   Phyllis and David York and Ted Wachtel, *Toughlove* (New York: Doubleday, 1982), 158.

8.   Hebrews 1:14

CHAPTER 7
SURVIVE AND THRIVE

1.   Wallerstein, *The Unexpected Legacy of Divorce.*

2.   Jude 23, TLB

3.   Matthew 25:35, 40

4.   Adapted from Bray and Kelly, *Stepfamilies,* 12.

5.   Wallerstein, *The Unexpected Legacy of Divorce,* 308.

BIBLIOGRAPHY

BOOKS THAT HELPED ME

Bray, Dr. James D. and John Kelly. *Stepfamilies: Love, Marriage, and Parenting in the First Decade.* New York: Broadway Books, 1998.

Cole, Edwin Louis. Everything he ever wrote; that's my dad!

Crabb, Larry. *Basic Principles of Christian Counseling.* Grand Rapids, MI: Zondervan Publishing House, 1975.

Curran, Dolores. *Traits of a Healthy Family.* San Francisco: Harper SanFrancisco, 1983.

Dobson, James, Ph.D. *Dare to Discipline.* Wheaton, IL: Tyndale House, 1970.

Glenn, H. Stephen, Ph.D. and Jane Nelson, Ed.D. *Raising Self-Reliant Children in a Self-Indulgent World.* Roseville, CA: Prima Publishing, 2000.

Harley, Willard F., Jr. *His Needs, Her Needs: Building an Affair-Proof Marriage.* Grand Rapids, MI: Fleming H. Revell, 1986.

Martin, Judith. *Miss Manners' Guide for the Turn-of-the-Millennium.* New York: Pharos Books, 1989.

——. *Miss Manners' Guide to Excruciatingly Correct Behavior.* New York: Warner Books, Inc., 1982.

——. *Miss Manners' Guide to Rearing Perfect Children.* New York: Budget Book Service, Inc., 1997.

Nelson, Jane, Ed.D. *Positive Discipline.* Ballantine Books, 1987.

Parrott, Les, Ph.D. and Leslie Parrott, Ph.D. *Saving Your Marriage Before It Starts.* Grand Rapids, MI: Zondervan.

Roberts, Monty. *The Man Who Listens to Horses.* New York: Random House, 1996.

Savage, Karen and Patricia Adams. *The Good Stepmother.* New York: Avon Books, 1989.

212

Bibliography

Seixas, Judith S. and Geraldine Youcha. *Children of Alcoholism: A Survivor's Manual.* New York: Harper and Row, 1985.

Sledge, Tim. *Making Peace With Your Past.* Nashville, TN: LifeWay Press, 1992.

Pidgeon, Mary Jean. *The Purpose, Power and Position of a Woman.* Shippensburg, PA: Destiny Image, 1998.

Wallerstein, Judith, Ph.D. *The Unexpected Legacy of Divorce.* New York: Hyperion, 2000.

OTHER BOOKS THAT MAY HELP

Burns, Cherie. *Stepmotherhood: How to Survive Without Feeling Frustrated, Left Out or Wicked.* New York: Harper and Row, 1986.

Barnett, Tommy. *There's a Miracle in Your House.* Lake Mary, FL: Creation House, 1993.

Chapman, Gary. *Five Signs of a Functional Family.* Chicago: Northfield Publishing, 1997.

———. *The Five Love Languages.* Chicago: Northfield Publishing, 1995.

Conwell, Russell H. *Acres of Diamonds.* n.c., Jove Publishing, 1995 (reissue edition).

Faulkner, Paul, Ph.D. *Achieving Success Without Failing Your Family.* West Monroe, LA: Howard Publishing, 1994.

Gottman, John, Ph.D. *Why Marriages Succeed or Fail.* New York: Simon and Schuster, 1994.

Harley, Willard F., Jr. *Love Busters: Overcoming the Habits That Destroy Romantic Love.* Grand Rapids, MI: Fleming H. Revell, 1997.

Kesler, Jay. *Too Big to Spank.* Regal Books, 1978.

Leman, Kevin, Ph.D. *Living in a Stepfamily Without Getting Stepped On.* Nashville, TN: Thomas Nelson, 1994.

Norwood, Perdita Kirkwood. *The Enlightened Stepmother.* New York: Avon Books, 1999.

Whitfield, Charles L., M.D. *Co-Dependence: Healing the Human Condition.* Deerfield Beach, FL: Health Communications, Inc., 1991.

York, Phyllis and David and Ted Wachtel. *Toughlove.* New York: Doubleday, 1982.

WE WOULD LOVE TO KNOW IF OUR STORY HELPED YOU,
SO PLEASE FEEL FREE TO WRITE TO EITHER OR BOTH OF US.
WE ARE ALSO AVAILABLE FOR STEPFAMILY WORKSHOPS.

JOANN OR SETH WEBSTER
P.O. BOX 3282
GRAPEVINE, TX 76099